Juvenile Justice in Double Jeopardy:

The Distanced Community and Vengeful Retribution

Juvenile Justice in Double Jeopardy:

The Distanced Community and Vengeful Retribution

Justine Wise Polier

LEA LAWRENCE ERLBAUM ASSOCIATES, PUBLISHERS

1989   Hillsdale, New Jersey   Hove and London

Lawrence Erlbaum Associates, Inc., Publishers
365 Broadway
Hillsdale, New Jersey 07642

Library of Congress Cataloging in Publication Data

Polier, Justine Wise, 1903-1987.
    Juvenile justice in double jeopardy.

    Includes index.
    1. Juvenile justice, Administration of--New York (State)--History. 2. Juvenile courts--New York (State)--History. 3. Juvenile justice, Administration of--United States--History. 4. Juvenile courts--United States--History. I. Title.
KFN6195.P65 1989   345.747'081   88-24409
ISBN 0-8058-0462-5

Printed in the United States of America
5 4 3 2 1

To Shad,

whose wisdom in law, battles for human rights,
and boundless love for others
served as goad and inspiration.

Contents

Foreword

Robert H. Bremner

"I feel a lot of hate, I know it's for myself, but I try to put it on others. ... All I want is two people I could never have.... Foster parents get paid for taking care of us. That's not love.... I'm afraid to be on my own.... I don't know how to make anything of myself ... I can't get a job—what am I going to do, talk like I talk in the street? That's all I know. I can't even read the forms ... I don't even know who my caseworker is. I don't know who my social worker is ... I don't even know where I was born."[1]

The speaker, Mercedes Colon, has spent 13 of her 18 years in foster care. Her parents, so she has been told, are dead. She does not know who took care of her until she was 5, and she cannot remember how many foster homes she has lived in. She has never felt loved or wanted. Who is responsible for letting a neglected child grow up in such a negligent way?

Justine Wise Polier's deeply felt and vigorously argued book helps us understand how broadly shared responsibility for Mercedes' neglect is and how profoundly we must reshape our attitudes and realign our priorities if we sincerely want to help the thousands of children like her who are dependent on the public for care and support.

Much of the book is based on Justice Polier's observations and experiences from the mid-1930s to 1973 as Judge of the Domestic Relations Court and New York State Family Court in New York City. The author's memories, however, extend back to a pre-World War I childhood, college and law school in the 1920s, and legal work for New York State and City in the Depression. For many years she was a director of the Field Foundation, a leader in philanthropic efforts for child welfare and betterment of interracial and intercultural relations, and since 1973 she worked with the Children's Defense Fund in its advocacy for children and youth. Incidents drawn from all these sources enrich and enliven the account of the granting and denial of justice to juveniles in 20th-century America, and inform her analyses of the strengths and weaknesses of public and private systems involved in the juvenile justice process. Justice Polier's long record of service for children adds urgency to her warning of "an ominous crisis in the future well-being of this country" stemming from society's neglect of and hostility to the poor in general and poor children in particular.

Readers will be particularly interested in Justice Polier's comments on, and assessment of, the Juvenile Court. By the 1930s when Polier joined the Court, its once-bright image had become tarnished. Contrary to the expectation of the founders, Juvenile Courts had become poor people's courts with poor facilities, poor funding, heavy caseloads, overworked and underpaid staffs, and judges accorded low status in the judicial hierarchy. Nevertheless the concept of the court as an agency to help children, whether dependent, neglected, or delinquent, survived and remains alive today. In discussing her years on the bench, Polier cites examples of "the endless discrepancies between principles and actual practices affecting juvenile delinquents" and calls attention to "the perpetual lack of adequate services" available to the court and its clientele, the arbitrary power exercised by voluntary agencies in accepting or rejecting children referred by the court, and "conflicts among those with power to make decisions." She also calls attention to people like Dr. Helen Montague, Dr. Marion E. Kenworthy, and Charles Schinitsky who, in different ways, made important contributions to the work of the court. In her judgment the court has been weakened by the loss of direct contact with delinquent and neglected children and diminished discretion and responsibility for dispositions of its cases. Her emphasis is always on provision of appropriate services to children in trouble and she has sharp words for those who would deny needed services on "law and order" or libertarian grounds or curtail them for budgetary reasons.

Distancing is a theme that runs through the book. It means putting oneself or an institution, like the court, in a position where it is difficult to see the consequences of actions or inaction. Distancing can be self-imposed by ignorance or indifference or it can be brought about by impersonal factors such as well-intentioned but short-sighted reforms that shift decision making to higher echelons and reduce the authority of workers in close touch with the problem. Justice Polier cites numerous examples of how distancing has affected (deformed is her word) juvenile justice and pervades both public and private agencies responsible for caring for neglected and delinquent children. The case of Mercedes Colon, mentioned previously, illustrates the results of distancing in public care of a neglected child.

The message that comes through most clearly in *Juvenile Justice in Double Jeopardy* is the need for humility and respect in dealing with difficult human problems. Polier speaks of "painful and humbling lessons," "myths supported by pride and fear," judicial decisions marked by "uncertainty and pretensions to wisdom," "swift, punitive justice" that held "too easy virtue for judges," and "self-righteousness" in the Reagan administration's policy toward delinquent youth. She calls for closer attention to the "underlying causes giving rise to violence in this country," harder efforts to understand delinquents and their parents, "wider respect and support from the larger community for unmarried parents," and urges reformers to resist the tendency to oversimplify what needs to be done without sufficient regard to the problems of individual children.

Respect and consideration for others cannot be achieved by fiat. Law, depending on the way it is written, applied, and interpreted, can compel respect or condone violation of the rights of others. Justice Polier asks us not only to respect the rights of the poor and troublesome children but to recognize their vulnerability and promise. The great enemies of respect and consideration for any individual or group are ignorance, arrogance, and prejudice. Justine Wise Polier fought these forces throughout her career and she continues to attack them in this remarkable book.

Preface

Judges are judged each day by those who come before them and by their associates. Yet, judging oneself and how much one achieves is easily postponed. Probing what is being done in the name of justice for children and youth has become a more urgent task as attacks are mounted against securing substantive justice through the courts. Past and present failures of the Juvenile Court are entangled with dependence on many systems of care and punishment.

Judges are not alone in avoiding self-examination. At the joyous celebration of the Statue of Liberty on July 4, 1986, the President and other public figures extolled America's commitment to liberty. Millions of citizens shared a glow of pride in the goodness of their heritage. The absence of blacks, Puerto Ricans, and those now denied sanctuary in this country went all but unnoticed. Only the poetic words on the statue spoke of the huddled poor yearning to be free. A similar loss of historic perspective now threatens the search for juvenile justice.

It is over 20 years since Myrdal first described the underclass in this country as composed of the unemployed, who became unemployables and eventually hopeless. He envisioned the injuries to their children. Today the phrase is used frequently, but the injuries persist with little understanding of the erosion of life for youths who have lost hope for their future.

In what now seems a simpler period, as we look back, the Juvenile Court movement of the late 19th century tells of a very small band of people moved to aid neglected children and return delinquent children to life in society. In that period of optimism for the future, the founders believed these two objectives could be joined as never before. They were united in their insistence that children must be removed from criminal trials and rescued from imprisonment with adults. Legislatures and communities in state after state followed their lead. The subsequent history of these courts has been far more ambiguous. It tells of irrational seesaws that have moved poor children up generous slides and down hostile slopes.

As the Juvenile Court, contrary to the expectations of its founders, became an institution only for the poor, the court, like the youths before it, became increasingly segregated from other institutions. Gradually, the positive optimism of the 19th century gave way to negative pessimism. In the past decade, the speed of this process has been accelerated by growing disregard for the poor. Self-doubt and fear have reduced efforts to meet the problems of youths characterized as part of the underclass. The confidentiality of the Juvenile Court, intended to protect children, has yielded to public exposure of youths as criminal offenders. The doctrine of doing less is extolled from on high as doing more. Concern for "the family" is presented as a goal that justifies reduced intervention on behalf of children neglected or abused behind family walls. As the underclass is accepted as a fixture in American society, youths—as a major group within it—receive less and less attention, except when they commit serious offenses.

As I visited hospitals, child-care institutions, shelters, and detention centers, despite their overcrowding or large number of children, there were always some staff who had become deeply moved by the magic touch of a specific child. Something between the child and adult had stirred the adult from daily routine to deep feeling for the child.

Why or how this happened was beyond explanation. Why it was limited to one child was baffling. Once such a relationship occurred, the child had created an advocate. This was true in court. Some children drew adoptive parents, teachers, court workers to their aid, whereas others passed almost unnoticed. I recall children who broke through procedure and challenged every court routine so that the judge moved down from the bench and closer to the child to discover what might be done. Then there were all the others for whom remembrance as well as action had become dim forgetfulness.

Spotty solicitude in every institution secured benefits for individual children, but it was no substitute for a comprehensive system of care that could provide more than a chance break for a few youth.

Despite, or because of, the accelerated withdrawal of support for youths and the myths that have removed them from the agenda of our conscience, I have written of the granting and denial of justice I observed while on the bench. My picture may seem primitive, but it is neither simple nor abstract.

It describes private and public systems that have granted or restricted help, the perpetual lack of adequate services, the problems inherent in a poor man's court and the conflicts among those with power to make decisions. I have tried to paint an honest picture of the youths before the court and of those charged with deciding their fate.

Americans have long been proud of being a child-centered, if not child-spoiling, society. But we have rarely taken stock of the vast differences in the ways we cherish our own children, yet judge children who look or act in ways we dislike or disapprove. Caring for children and demands for their conformity have run on parallel tracks, generally meeting only at time of personal or community crises.

At this time, the spread of poverty and unemployment among youth warns of an ominous crisis in the future well-being of this country. New battle lines, not yet formed, have begun to appear. The drive for greater punishment, the transfer of more youthful offenders at younger ages to the Criminal Court system, and the further reduction of public aid appear as today's judgments. The Department of Justice has turned its back on youth and supports only more secure incarceration and the building of more prisons. This is part of the wider government policy to further strip safety nets for the poor.

At the same time, other voices question these policies. They ask why, as statistics show a drop in crime and delinquency, are more arrests being made. They ask why youths are being taken directly or by waiver to adult jails. They ask what happens to these youths before and after criminal court trials. They question the lack of training for employment in places of confinement. Finally, they ask about the disproportionate incarceration of poor minority youth and how they are selected for punishment.[1]

Arthur Schlesinger Jr. has written about the cycles in American history that move from public to private interest and back again. In the field of child care and justice such cycles also appear. From loving concern for infants to a more remote relationship, institutions have evolved that have become increasingly impersonal. Today, there is the beginning of a new cycle that recognizes the value of personal relations in a child's life as well as order in the many systems of care. How they will be meshed is the challenge for the future of this country and its youth. Compassionate gatekeepers in child care, as in medicine, are essential to make services meaningful. This will take time.

Regardless of the need for finding new ways of securing justice for youth, a fresh look and new ardor are needed to discover how this country's vast resources can be used to assure substantive justice for all its children.

Acknowledgments

There is no way to speak of or even recall the many men, women, and children to whom I feel deeply grateful. It is only possible to mention a few whose lives and friendships brought me the rarest of gifts.

To have been born in Portland, Oregon, when it was still part of "the wild West" and to have chosen as my family a loving mother and father, who were among the first of progressive parents, and a vibrant older brother, were double blessings. An unorthodox education, work in a textile town, and study at Yale Law School brought friends and the belief that law could be used as an instrument to challenge injustice. After appointment as a referee in the New York State Department of Labor and a study of Public Welfare in New York, assignment to the Juvenile Court as "the first woman judge" in New York seemed only a temporary post. But it captured and held me for nearly four decades. Each day revealed the miseries and the strengths of those brought before the bench. Concealed enemies and caring colleagues were part of each day's work.

During my first years on the court, two judges, one a charming puritan, Lawrence Dunham, and the other Rosalie Loew Whitney, steeped in social problems, never tired in their efforts to help the many families and children struck down in Depression days. As the court grew, Mayor LaGuardia appointed some remarkable judges: Hubert Delany, Jane Bolin, and the learned Dudley Sicher. We became close allies in fighting religious bigotry and opposing institutional racism, before that term gained currency. Later Louis Otten, Sylvia Liese, and Nanette Dembitz became working colleagues in this group. Without these friends and colleagues, life in the court would have been a lonely assignment. With them, although we were often in a minority at meetings of the Board of Justices, there was no thought of giving up.

Besides these colleagues, there were always members of the court staff who welcomed possibilites for going beyond the routine duties of their work. Without professional training, a few of the "old-timers" had the gift of reaching out to children and parents that lessened fears and even healed old wounds. They were aided by a small group of unusual volunteers who visited homes in the most desolate areas of the city for more than 20 years. These were the dedicated foot soldiers who made judging more than a ceremony.

One other important source of aid to the court came from a few leaders in the mental health professions, who volunteered their services to proba-tion officers, agency staff and to those judges who welcomed them. Among them, Dr. Marion E. Kenworthy, Dr. Viola W. Bernard, and Dr. Max Win-sor led all the rest. They provided new insights into human behavior, proposed ways to meet problems beyond traditional court lines, and gave their time without thought of recompense.

An old friend and eminent member of the bar, Louis Weiss, brought me the friendship of Marshall and Ruth Field. On moving to New York, Mr. Field wanted to explore how he could best use his wealth to help children in this city. Unlike most philanthropists, he wanted to study and learn before he acted. Together with a creative educator, Agnes King Inglis, he spent many months visiting institutions and homes, and sitting with me in the Juvenile Court. Staff members did not recognize him, but one delinquent boy announced after Mr. Field had left court, "I know that man. His picture was in *LIFE* magazine." Slowly, with keen judgment and rare modesty, Mr. Field provided new possibilities for better care, and challenged the long ac-cepted discrimination that had excluded black children from foster care and adoptive homes.

When the Field Foundation was established in 1941, it also undertook work in other parts of the country. As a member of its board, I was able to present problems seen from the bench, and I learned much from its early directors, Maxwell Hahn and Leslie Dunbar. They traveled widely from the deep South to Indian country and to the ghettos of northern cities. They un-covered problems and presented programs for children who were suffering poverty, hunger, and discrimination. With the help of a group of concerned physicians, Dunbar led the way in exposing hunger and malnutrition in the United States.

On leaving the bench, I was able to travel and see more of what was being done for youth in other parts of this country and in other lands. During this same period, new ways of collecting and interpreting data raised questions about old assumptions, while pretensions to the use of these new skills sometimes produced absurdities. A series of volumes were replete with descriptions of gremlins in the operation of courts and child welfare, but the authors were generally remote from the youth about whom they wrote. Recently some treatises about youthful offenders have reverted to genetic theories and asserted the responsibility of individual youth, distanced and unobserved by the authors.

In this period of reducing aid to poor youth while holding them accountable individually, direct observations of people within and outside the court seem especially relevant. The youths, their families, and those intended to help them are not shadows or ghosts to be banished from sight.

In writing, I have drawn primarily on the experience of 37 years as a judge, reading and court decisions. I also reviewed some 500 case records which I had put aside because they told of my failures and inability to do what seemed needed for individual children. The cases cited are not a random sample. Rather they have been presented to illustrate how the court, public welfare, and social agencies responded to children brought before the court over four decades. During this period (1935 to 1972), changing public policies affected the administration of juvenile justice as they did all social institutions.

It is not possible to give credit to the many sources of ideas and knowledge gleaned from reading. However, I must express special appreciation to Professor Robert Bremner, from whose unique *Children and Youth in America: A Documentary History* of childhood since 1600 I learned so much. I am deeply grateful that this eminent scholar agreed to critique my manuscript, to make valuable suggestions, and to write the Foreword.

In reviewing and organizing large numbers of decisions, notes and many court records, Luba Lynch, my assistant, was of invaluable aid. I am grateful to Nancy Miller, who helped in the editing, and to Jeanette Murawski and Anne Volpe who typed and retyped sections graciously without complaint. Cornelia Bessie, my wise, skillful editor and loving friend, was most responsible for making me bring together the many bits and pieces that present the puzzles of court life. She knew when to prod and when to let go as my pace slowed or quickened, and our friendship deepened through our work together.

Finally, unstinting support from my husband, Shad Polier, was central to my work throughout all my years on the bench. His creative approach to law, driven by a restless conscience in the face of injustice, never lagged. His hard, searching questions were loving in spirit. His analytical skills resulted in major legislative changes that freed many children from traditional, harmful enclosures. For his limitless gifts of self and for the sympathetic interest of our children, Stephen, Trudy, and Jonathon, no words can express my debt.

Justine Wise Polier
New York City, December 1986

Justine Wise Polier died on July 31, 1987. Shortly before her death, she had completed the manuscript of this book. References were incomplete, however. I am very grateful to Elizabeth Schack for helping me with the task of locating the full citations. Unfortunately, a few could not be found. Many helpful suggestions also were made by Viola W. Bernard, MD. I am also deeply indebted to Kathleen Kelly, Ph.D. who, with energy and devotion, made it possible to prepare the manuscript for publication. Finally, I want to thank the Board of Directors of the Kenworthy-Swift Foundation for their support in this effort.

Trudy Festinger
July 1988

Chapter 1
Fifty Years of Changing Political Winds

For an intimate observer of any institution, there is always risk of exaggerating the obvious and not noting the less strident factors that make up the landscape. Yet, that risk is worth taking if it provides a portrait of what has gone on in the minds and actions of judges and the lives of youth rather than a photograph or set of statistical tables. Each decade for 50 years had had its ups and downs controlled by forces far beyond the administration of justice for children and youth in New York and throughout the country. Regardless of its virtues or faults, the Juvenile Courts have served as a sensitive barometer of community attitudes and political action that have governed the lives of millions of poor men, women, and children during the past half century.

Before the Creation of the Juvenile Court

Providing generously for children who are wards of the State has not been a popular public policy.[1]

Law and practice enforced the "work ethic" harshly on poor children in early America. There were few who, with Thomas Jefferson, saw that premature labor of children presented the "flattering appearance of their being men while they were yet children, but ending in reducing them to be children when they should be men." Being "tightfisted" toward the children of the poor was long regarded as a virtue, and reforms for poor children were couched in moralistic terms. Saving children through charity, protecting morality through discipline, and providing safeguards for property provided yeast for each recipe.

At the Creation

The Juvenile Court in the 1890s promised a clean break with the past. It would treat children as different from adults. Children would be removed from contact with adult offenders. The court was to discover and meet the needs of each neglected or dependent child. It was to discover why a child was moving down a delinquent path and redirect him.[2] The Juvenile Court judge was to be different from other judges. In the words of one of its eminent founders, Judge Julian W. Mack, the judge was to act as a wise, kindly, and effective parent. It was even envisioned that the replacement of punishment by rehabilitation of children would provide a new model for individualized justice to the adult Criminal Court system.

At law school in the 1920s this enticing picture of the opportunity to do justice was not marred by the realities that shadowed the vision. No one spoke of the staggering caseloads, of the niggardly resources provided by states, of the powerful forces that had bent the court to comply with the status quo, of racial injustice, or of the double standard of morality for the poor and the nonpoor. The absence of social legislation was still a source of pride in this country.

Before the 1930 epoch of law and social action, the Juvenile Court held out special charms. Legislation in Illinois had authorized the court to provide aid to poor children in their homes under the doctrine of *parens patriae*, or the state as a substitute parent,[3] although this program was attacked as an entering wedge for socialism. The judges were not to be cloaked in robes. They were to sit at a table with children and parents rather than look down from on high. They were to call on the burgeoning social sciences for guidance in decision making. Unlike the august Chancery Court in England, the Juvenile Court in the United States would not limit its jurisdiction to children with property.

After a few years as a referee in Workmen's Compensation (the first social legislation to be held constitutional) and as counsel to the Emergency Relief Bureau in New York, I believed that the Juvenile Court would offer an oasis in the legal landscape. It took time to realize that the Juvenile

Court was an insignificant off-shore island in the eyes of the higher echelons of the judiciary system, the organized bar, and officials who appropriated funding. There was little general interest except when a shocking case of physical abuse or violent delinquency was leaked to the press. The oasis had become a desert populated only by the very poor and a small band of people designated to aid them. Only a few benevolent tourists came from time to time, but they did not stay for long. The urgent problems of each day, at first, obscured how powerful political trade winds determined what a Juvenile Court could or would try to do.

One bequest to juvenile justice survived from the Elizabethan Poor Law of 1662 that denied aid to poor children without legal residence in a state. In 1964, half of the states in this country still had compulsory removal statutes for nonresidents "who were or were likely to become public charges," and 39 states had residence requirements for welfare assistance. Under reciprocal state agreements, delinquent youths were denied the opportunity to live with relatives in other states who were ready and eager to receive them. Similar restrictions were used against the movement of neglected and dependent children.

In 1965, the mother of Jane, aged 3, had died. Her father was in prison under a long sentence and there was no one in New York to care for her. Cousins took her directly from the mother's funeral to their home in Michigan, but that state demanded that the Juvenile Court in New York provide a bond that she would not become a dependent, under threat of returning her to New York. The New York Department of Welfare agreed that a bond was required under an interstate compact.[4] When I refused to sign the bond, as an unconstitutional interference with this child's right to travel, Michigan threatened to appeal but did not do so. Jane was later adopted by her Michigan cousins.

Such bans to prevent poor children from moving across state lines had been continued despite a 1941 Supreme Court decision that a California statute making it a crime to bring an indigent person into the state violated the commerce clause.[5] At that time, however, it was only the concurring opinion of Justice Douglas (joined by Justices Black and Murphy) that proclaimed the right of Americans to travel freely. This viewpoint was slow to affect the decisions of welfare departments and Juvenile Courts that dealt with poor children.

A Poor Man's Court

> The support of the poor is in all countries a burden, and the object of legislators is to make that burden as little felt by the industrious citizens as possible.[6]

Traditional attitudes toward the poor reached into every crevice in the administration of juvenile justice. Parents seeking aid and youth charged with offenses sat for hours in airless waiting rooms. Noisy verbal and physical battles had to be broken up by court attendants. The hard benches on which everyone was forced to sit and the atmosphere, like that in lower Criminal Courts, resembled bullpens more than a court for human beings. When air conditioners were introduced they were first installed in courtrooms and judicial chambers, rather than in the stifling waiting rooms.

The workload of a judge, often 100 cases a day in the 1930s, demanded speedy dispositions of the living poor, not unlike disposition of the dead during a plague. Because it was assumed that any judge could do justice to a child, the rotation of judges allowed shuffling of a child's case among as many as a dozen judges over a period of months. The child became known to court attendants but was a stranger to each judge—just one more child slipped into and lost in an ever fattening court file. Like the youngest child in a big family, delinquent and neglected children were served the leftovers from the table of justice.[7]

Juvenile Courts were bowed down by disabilities imposed by law and custom on all institutions for the poor. They were often lodged in old, ramshackle buildings. Decor and decorum were lacking. In 1964, a distinguished newspaper commentator, after visiting the New York Family Court, wrote: "It is a poor man's court. Lawyers are rare and courtrooms are bare, toilet walls are defaced. The court's waiting rooms resemble those at hospital clinics. Negro and Puerto Rican families predominate, and many regard the trappings of justice with bitterness or suspicion."[8]

From its inception, Juvenile Court judges were also subjected to discriminatory treatment. They received less compensation than judges appointed or elected to other courts. They were given no law clerks and were not expected to write opinions. In New York, neither law reports nor legal periodicals were provided for their use. Until the 1960s the only book provided in each part of the court was the Gideon Bible presented by a devout Lutheran colleague.

Most destructive was the scarcity of personnel to work with children or families. Professionally trained staff were few in number. Although probation officers were described as guides, philosophers, and friends to youth, they too were demeaned. Their compensation was below that for sanitation workers as well as for probation officers in other courts, and there were few qualifications required for their work. The National Council on Crime and Delinquency (NCCD) survey in the 1960s reported that 8% of the counties in the United States had no minimum educational requirements for probation officers, 14% required only high school graduation, and 74% required college graduation but no specialized preparation. Only 4% required a graduate degree.

Few courts had probation officers to work with delinquent children returned home after placement, a strategic time to help them readjust to community life. A national study by the National Council on Crime and Delinquency reported that it was not uncommon for 250 children to be assigned to two or three after-care staff.

Subtle undermining of juvenile justice was condoned by both the higher judiciary and the bar. Words of appreciation for the work of the Juvenile Court were largely limited to ceremonial occasions. They offered no more lasting benefits than Thanksgiving baskets for the poor. In 1956, after studying how to improve the courts in New York State, the Temporary Commission agreed that the time of State Supreme Court judges was too valuable to spend on Family Court issues. In this same period the jurisdiction of the Family Court was enlarged to relieve the Supreme Court of some burdensome cases involving support and custody issues. One Appellate judge told that the first advice given by colleagues, when he went on the State Supreme Court, was to avoid custody cases, because once assigned, they pursued the judge forever.

In their isolation from the problems of youth before the Family Court, the higher judicial hierarchy generally focused on administrative reforms that would not require substantial new funding for services. The response of the Family Court administration to demands for greater efficiency was to create separate parts for preliminary hearings, for neglect and delinquency cases, for child abuse cases, for adoption, for review of placements, for termination of parental rights, and for youths charged with felonies. Such "reforms" negated the promise of comprehensive treatment of all family problems envisioned by the Family Court Act of 1962.

Political Winds

As an insignificant part of the judiciary, the Juvenile Court was especially vulnerable to shifting winds, whether favorable or hostile to the poor.

In the 1930s well-meant requests that a child be removed from the family home only because of poverty were constant. Like other judges, I felt forced to acquiesce, knowing that such actions had neither justification nor any alternative. A self-rescue operation allowed me to concentrate on the small number of cases in which I could secure aid without disruption of families mired in despair. Later, as New Deal legislation provided aid for more children in their own homes, happier endings were made possible.

To challenge traditional abuses of power exercised by public officials as well as charitable organizations that demanded compliance with their rules remained an ongoing necessity. On a single court day, children in four families were brought before the court for placement. In the first, the family had suffered eviction because of an error by the welfare district, an error it had failed to correct. In the second, welfare had been suspended due to conflicting, unchecked medical reports about the father's ability to work. In the third, welfare had been refused because the welfare district believed a widowed mother must have had other resources because she had waited "too long" to seek aid after losing her job. This proud woman had waited until she had sold her last piece of furniture. In the fourth case, the mother of two children had dared to report that the welfare worker had demanded a bribe. Each case demanded long questioning by the judge to secure a return of welfare aid and to prevent removal of the children.

Some judges felt such investigatory procedures from the bench were not an appropriate function for a judge. They, also, had little patience for judges who sat for long hours listening to the miseries of those who came before them, when there was so little they could do. They remained aloof from the few activist judges who appeared at legislative hearings to seek more adequate budgets or who joined citizen groups to battle against racial discrimination. Differences in viewpoints on the proper role of the judge were smothered by a polite silence on substantive problems in discussions with one another.

The 1940s: War and Demands for Conformity

The 1940s were not auspicious years for justice to poor children. With preparation for war and the coming of war, more fathers were enlisted in the armed services, and more mothers and fathers went to work. There was little interest in the growing numbers of neglected and delinquent children left to fend for themselves. Staff in the courts were depleted. Even Mayor LaGuardia, generally sympathetic to the needs of children, rejected funding mental health services with the curt comment that children needed Borden-Sheffield (milk) rather than Binet-Simon (psychological tests). Deterioriation of services became so widespread that one distinguished federal administrator found it necessary to urge the individual states to do more to help parents and relatives care for children in times of family stress.[9]

Demands for proof of patriotism and conformity during this period reached the courts in many ways. The Acting Presiding Justice[10] in New York rejected desperately needed volunteers from a Harlem organization, saying that the leader of this group had been an "extremely tenacious witness" in a case he had heard 1 year earlier.[11] When children rioted against outrageous conditions at the Manhattan Society for the Prevention of Cruelty to Children, they were carted off, without notice to families, to an adult jail at night by order of this same judge. A well-qualified applicant for a civil service position in probation was rejected on the grounds that he had been a conscientious objector. The Court Administrator wrote that returning veterans were better suited to inspire youth with "patriotism and self-restraint."[12]

Attacks on welfare recipients intensified soon after the end of the war. Unmarried mothers and their children were special targets for contempt. At one meeting of charitable women, after I had spoken about the injustice of attacks against mothers on ADC, Dick Gregory, engaged to entertain the group, stopped on his way to the platform. He shocked the comfortable audience by announcing: "I am an ADC child." He then told how his struggling mother had brought home a pair of shoes discarded by a boy who had outgrown them. The next morning he proudly put on his first good shoes as he got ready for school. But, his mother told him to take them off, saying, "If anyone sees you in those shoes, they'll be sure I'm working and we'll lose our aid." He took them off without a word, and put on his worn sneakers.

Charitable ladies were not alone in feeling discomfort when faced with new perceptions of old needs, or with the assertion of new rights for poor people.

Public services for dependent and neglected children were opposed in New York by voluntary agencies while hundreds of well babies were held in city hospitals waiting for foster care. Black children were the hardest hit. In June 1949, the Juvenile Court in New York was advised by its chief probation officer that "unless a child is in a hospital or a very undesirable shelter such as the Municipal Lodging House, it will be foolish to refer Negro children to foster care programs."

With sharply declining revenues, charitable agencies felt overwhelmed. Their way of meeting the situation was to limit intake of children while still insisting on their traditional right to select those whom they chose to help. As early as 1947, at a meeting of the Citizens' Committee for Children of New York, Mrs. Roosevelt warned that the attacks on children and families dependent on welfare were only symptoms of a far more serious congressional threat to many social programs.

The 1950s: A Period of Retreat

After World War I, legislation to improve the health of mothers and infants had been opposed by the American Medical Association as part of a "socialist scheme."[13] After World War II, the Mid-Century White House Conference on Children limited its proposals largely to opposing communist imperialism, to building character in youth, and to strengthening belief in God. It did not heed the 1940 conference warning that unless new knowledge about the causation and prevention of delinquency was put to work, the next decades would see an increase in rebellious and delinquent children.

All during the post-World War II period, problems stemming from social pathology or the violation of civil rights were brushed aside as having no importance except to "bleeding hearts" or radicals. Two incidents brought this home (to me) in personal ways. The State Department questioned my request for a renewal of my passport. It focused on my membership on a war-time committee to secure services for poor children and on my brother's authorship of a campaign biography of Henry Wallace. In court, when I questioned a new administrative practice of requesting information from public schools as to whether children before the court had been released to attend religious instruction, a colleague snapped, "This is a Christian country." None of my colleagues countered this pronouncement.

Stalwart courage of a few men and women stand out indelibly in my memory of the 1950s. On December 5, 1952, Marshall Field was called before the House Committee in Congress appointed to investigate foundations. He was questioned on why he had two persons, suspected of being "subversive," on the board of the Field Foundation. The first was Channing Tobias, a great American and distinguished black leader. Next he was questioned on my fitness to serve on the Foundation board, because I had been associated with three organizations cited by the House Un-American Activities Committee.[14] In straightforward words and with imperturbable grace, Mr. Field replied that he respected my work and my contributions to the Foundation board, and that he trusted me. He did not flinch. The Committee stopped its investigation of the Field Foundation at that time.

In contrast, members of the higher judicial hierarchy showed anxiety about a Juvenile Court judge acting as either a citizen or a judge to protect constitutional rights. One state Supreme Court judge said that he found my decision, dismissing charges of neglect against black parents who refused to send their children to segregated and inferior schools, interesting.[15] Then he added quickly that he did not agree with it. Asked for his reasons, he said I would be reversed by the Appellate Division and probably by the New York Court of Appeals. When I asked what position he thought the Supreme Court would take on the constitutional issues, he answered that the case would not reach that court. I told him that Thurgood Marshall (then Director of the National Education and Defense Fund) had called that morning to say that if my decision was appealed, the Fund would take the case all the way. "That makes it different" was the reply of the State judge.

Similar anxiety about independence of a Juvenile Court judge was reflected in two calls from the Presiding Justice of the Appellate Division. He inquired why several weeks had passed without my deciding the school segregation case, although longer delays were habitual on far less complex issues. The other call requested an explanation of why I had signed a citizen petition to abolish "witchhunting" by the "Un-American Activities Committee."

The most severe blow to an independent judiciary in New York came from Mayor Wagner in September 1955. He yielded to right-wing sectarian demands not to reappoint Judge Hubert Delany, despite the highest ratings by bar associations and citizen groups for two decades of exemplary service on the Family Court. The Mayor's explanation was that he did not agree with the political views of Judge Delany.

One of the few bright notes in the 1950s for youths before Juvenile Courts was the holding by Judge David Bazelon, senior judge of the Circuit Court of Appeals for the District of Columbia, that juveniles had a right to counsel.[16] This was a fitting prelude to the 1960s.

The 1960s: The Advent of Constitutional Rights for Minors

In juvenile justice and child welfare, the 1960 decade was one of eager excitement. The 1960 White House Conference faced realities for children who were nonwhite or who were born out of wedlock. It proclaimed that, "The Constitution itself was both racist and sexist in its conception. The greatest blemish on the history of the United States of America is slavery and its evil legacy." The conference also addressed what it called "a climate of fear which penetrates this nation." Delegates urged a new ingredient for youth problems—the treatment of youth with respect.

The application of the Bill of Rights to Juvenile Court procedures had enjoyed a distinguished, although sparse, ancestry. On the appeal of a father, over 100 years earlier, an Illinois Court reversed the commitment of a youth to a reformatory, asking why minors should "be deprived of liberty without due process of law."[17] However, the leading Juvenile Court case in 1932 had declared that the Court was not "seeking to punish the malefactor. It was seeking to salvage a boy,"[18] and therefore found the absence of due process justifiable. Little attention was paid for many years to the dissenting opinion of Judge Crane who had warned, "We must minimize the chance of abuse and place limitations even upon those who have the best of purposes and the most benevolent of dispositions."

Thirty more years passed before the New York State Legislature enacted a model Family Court Act (1962) requiring that children be represented in the Juvenile Court by counsel. It was largely a response to the writings of one able and concerned lawyer, Charles Schinitsky, whose studies on the need for counsel in the Children's Court had been published by the Bar Association of the City of New York.[19,20]

Five years later, the unanimous decisions of the Supreme Court and the ringing opinions of Justice Fortas in *Kent* (1966)[21] and in *Gault* (1967)[22] drove the right to due process into the Juvenile Courts. *Gault* established a child's entitlement to notice of charges, to counsel, to protection against self-incrimination, and to confront and produce witnesses. A few years later, the Supreme Court held that if a juvenile was charged with a criminal act, the level of proof must, as in criminal cases, be beyond a reasonable doubt.[23] However, the Supreme Court also held in another decision that the constitutional rights of minors did not require all the protections afforded in a criminal trial, and denied the constitutional right to a jury trial.[24] It was in this case that Justice Blackmun expressed the hope that the Juvenile Court would not be abandoned in favor of a return to Criminal Court proceedings.

The Application of Due Process Rights

The principle that the Bill of Rights was not for adults only and that children had the right to counsel gained wide acceptance in theory. Giving it content was a different matter. The quality of representation varied from state to state and within states.[25] During an out-of-state visit, I observed one judge conscientiously advising parents and youths of their rights. In the next county, a court clerk advised parents before they entered the courtroom that a child would do better before the judge if the parents waived the right to counsel.

In New York City, where funds were provided for full-time law guardians, legal representation was superior. Nevertheless, tensions ran high in the late 1960s and early 1970s when the period costumes of the public defenders—long straggly hair, ponytails, beads, and miniskirts—made them seem like guerilla warriors to many judges. It took time for judges to realize that the anger of these young advocates was not personal, but aimed against pretensions to justice, accepted too easily by judges. Slowly, law guardians and judges discovered common ground when they tackled substantive injustices stemming from lack of services or ongoing discriminatory practices.

Although the acceptance of due process proceeded, children and youth paid an unanticipated price for its benefits. Higher benches were raised between the judges and youths brought before the Juvenile Courts. Hands-on efforts to help youth by probation were restricted. Antiseptic distancing between court personnel and youth obscured their pain. Counsel bent on preventing intervention overlooked suffering that called for help. Like the accused man with a rope around his neck, for whom the judge demanded a trial before hanging, few youths in the ghettos won a new lease on life through due process. In court one could sense the bitterness of parents and of youth hurt by discrimination that dominated every aspect of their lives in school, in seeking work and on the streets—left unnoticed by the court and counsel.

The achievements of the drive for procedural due process were unable to stay the steady erosion of Federal efforts to grant substantive aid for poor youth that had been supported during the Kennedy administration and Johnson's "War on Poverty." The significant extension of Social Security, the expansion of day care for poor children and the enactment of Medicare in the mid-1970s are among the lasting memorials to that period—but no Secretary of Health, Education and Welfare since Ribicoff has publicly urged social workers to fight the slums, racial segregation, and the terrors of old age.[26]

Wars on the Poor, 1960 — 1986

Wars on the poor and their children have had a lasting power that few reforms can claim. As in military wars, the names of the leaders have changed. Yet, for nearly three decades, Richard Nixon, whether in or out of office, has led a macabre dance against poor youth and all those dependent on welfare. His major political goal has been to reduce the cost of welfare.

In 1961, Nixon denounced "people programs" as a warmed-over version of the old frontier. He contended then that government should concentrate on meeting the challenge of communism.[27] The words and tactics varied over the next 25 years, but the goal remained. In 1969 he had proposed a Family Assistance Plan to fix an annual ceiling of $1,500 for a "typical welfare family" of a mother and three children. There was no mention of fathers. As President in 1971, he was reported to have met in California with then-Governor Reagan and Caspar Weinberger, and agreed on a pilot project to allow states to waive protections for the poor required by Congressional entitlement programs.[28,29] That same year the administration proposed cuts in food allowances below its own low-budget diet and cuts in clinical, hospital, and narcotic programs. In this cutting season, one New York legislator even proposed the elimination of rat-control programs.

In 1971, when Congress enacted legislation authorizing more comprehensive services for poor children living in their own homes, President Nixon issued a devastating veto. He branded the legislation with the triple faults of fiscal irresponsibility, administrative unworkability, and family weakening. As one of the original California trio intent on reducing welfare aid, Caspar Weinberger, appointed to be Secretary of Health, Education and Welfare, became the grey eminence for the cutting programs. He undermined Congressional actions by impounding huge sums appropriated for poor children until enjoined by court actions.[30] Similar devices were adopted by Housing and Urban Development until they, too, were halted by court orders.

In October 1972, President Nixon announced at Independence Hall his signature to a bill that would institute "a new American revolution." By returning $30 billion to state and local governments, the New Federalism would restore power to the people. But these funds reached few poor families or their children. They were largely used to hold down local taxes and to increase police hardware. Only 8% of these funds were directed to social programs and only 1% went to aid children or youth in 1972.

The next step in the attacks against the poor took an added political turn. In 1973, regulations designed to safeguard welfare recipients against political harassment and violations of privacy were eliminated. The Director of Child and National Health Programs resigned that year, stating that the Nixon administration was not interested in the problems of children.[31] More cuts were on the drawing board for 1974 when President Nixon was forced to resign.

Prelude to the 1980s

Beginning with the 1967 State of the Union message, civil-rights and poverty issues practically disappeared from Presidential pronouncements, to be replaced by disquisitions on Safe Streets and Crime Control Acts, and other euphemisms for the forcible repression of black violence.[32]

Dehumanization of the poor spread during the Ford presidency, although in less strident fashion. Proposals to cut the food stamp program and to limit the cost-of-living allowances granted by social security were repeated. The Delinquency Prevention Act of 1974 shifted responsibility from the Federal government for preventive services, rehabilitation, and research in large part to the states. Congress did not provide the funding needed to enforce its mandate that noncriminal juvenile offenders be housed separately from adult criminals. For a time, Congress required that all welfare recipients enroll in job-training and work programs, even if they were the mothers of small children. The rejection by Congress of minimum standards for day care in 1974 was described by Professor Zigler of Yale as a blow quietly dealt to millions of poor children.[33]

By 1979, Professor Laurence Tribe concluded that special protection for the poor had been limited to fundamental rights and perhaps to only those "where equal protection would require no state expenditure." [34]

As in an aging turtle, the vital parts of child welfare programs had diminished as the encasing shell grew larger and thicker. New layers were added to the hard shell, by right-wing ideologues and by the subsequent fiscal restraints of the 1980s. The shell hid the miseries and problems of children surviving on AFDC benefits that were lower in the 1980s than a decade earlier. A national floor for such benefits had been defeated in Congress and there were no provisions that state benefits should be increased to meet inflation. Increasing rules and regulations to control costs drove many child-care workers out of the field.

More concern for the fundamental right of children to be free from abuse and discrimination was expressed by Congress in 1979, but there were few to challenge the words of Irving Kristol: "Don't throw money at problems."[35] This doctrine had become an excuse for doing less for adults and children in need.

The 1980s

The Reagan administration's first answer to poverty was sounded in January 1981 by David Stockman, then the new director of the Office of Management and Budget (OMB). In his first press conference, he called the Federal budget "an automatic soup kitchen stretching from coast to coast."[36] This comment foreshadowed the cutting of aid to the poor of all ages, including neglected children and delinquent youth. Official surgeons were put to work to excise social benefits and to develop new rules for depriving the poor of essential help.

A new strategy of secrecy was employed by the Federal government. The Office of Management and Budget assumed authority, not only to pass on the budgets of administrative departments, but also to impose silence upon the requests it rejected. When a study of the disproportionate rate of mortality among black infants was requested by the Department of Health and Human Services, it was rejected and the Department was directed not to disclose the request or the rejection. Only a "leak" brought the directive for silence to public attention.

The strategy of silence and secrecy obscured the problems of the poor from the larger community. Findings by the eminent physician, Dr. Raymond Wheeler, in 1979 had graphically presented the consequences of low birth weights among poor infants. He had testified that their susceptibility to infection, frequent illness, and poor school work was due to the malnutrition of their mothers during pregnancy. He also regarded many later employment and behavioral difficulties among these children as being due to malnutrition.[37] A few years earlier Dr. Brenner of Johns Hopkins had reported that the unemployment rate had substantially affected the physical health, mental health, and criminal aggression of the unemployed.[38] Such findings were not heard or welcomed.

In this period the new administration appeared blind to the fact that almost all youths charged with offenses in the Juvenile or Criminal Courts came from the vast pool of unemployed youth living in poverty. As described by Lloyd Ohlin, juvenile justice had moved from a development model in the 1950s to one focusing on controlling crime and from that to an eye-for-an-eye model in the 1980s.[39]

Willful ignorance, hostility, and the drive for fiscal restraint gave powerful support to every myth against the poor. Although the old myths that the poor suffered less when ill and therefore needed less medical care were no longer voiced aloud, inferior medical services for the poor, whether old or young, remained standard procedure. Special targets for attack ranged from food stamps to public housing and the unmarried mother. While some sincere concern was shown for the adequacy of parenting by a single parent, there was greater concern that single parents would produce generational poverty. This assumption overlooked the evidence that two-thirds of the female-headed families had lived in poverty before their children were born.

The Spread of Unemployment

In 1982, CETA, the major vestige of the Federal employment programs for youth, was abandoned, despite the sharp rise in unemployment. The following April, Dr. Alice Rivlin testified in Congress that one of every four youths under 18 was living in poverty.[40] It was twice as high for minority youths, with nearly half (46.7%) of black youths and more than a third of Hispanic youths living in poverty that year.[41] Yet it was not until the fall of 1985 that the press headlined the conditions of unemployed youth in America. In October 1985, the front page of *The New York Times* announced that the existence of "poor youth in an affluent nation was seen by experts as a new kind of social revolution with unpredictable ramifications."[42]

Interest in youth unemployment again all but disappeared from the media while Federal officials contended that there was virtually no relationship between economic conditions and an increase in criminal offenses.

The Role of the Courts

Throughout the past 50 years, the Juvenile Courts have largely paddled their leaking canoes with only occasional directives from the Federal Courts or State Appellate Courts. The 1960 revolution, establishing the right of youth to the protection of procedural due process, unleashed Federal Courts to correct or mitigate wrongful treatment of youths. Some Federal Courts examined with new care the condition of state institutions that held children or adults. They directed that shocking conditions be corrected. When unable to secure change, some Federal judges threatened the release of prisoners. In 1971 one district judge in Arkansas wrote:

> This court, of course, cannot require the voters to make available the resources needed to meet Constitutional standards, but it can and must require the release of persons held under conditions which violate their Constitutional rights.[43]

This search for substantive justice by the lower Federal Courts was short-lived. The United States Supreme Court, under Chief Justice Burger, looked with a jaundiced eye at lower Federal decisions that went beyond issues of procedural due process. In the Supreme Court decision upholding the denial of Federal funds for abortions, Justice Blackmun dissented, writing, "There truly is another world out there, the existence of which the Court, I suspect, either chooses to ignore or fears to recognize." But, the majority held that poverty standing alone (unlike racial discrimination) was not entitled to special scrutiny.

Juvenile Courts have trudged along. Whether satisfied or not, they have accepted the distancing of children and youth brought before them for aid or correction. As the benches grew taller each youth appeared smaller.

Chapter 2
For Delinquents: The Tail End of Justice

The juvenile delinquent has been the centerpiece of juvenile justice since its earlier days. However, never fully confident of what rehabilitation could achieve—legislatures issued conflicting directives. They set various age limits for jurisdiction and excluded the most serious offenses. Other limitations have been expanded since the 1970s, first through waiver systems to the Criminal Courts and second, by a dramatic increase in recriminalization of more and younger youth in the 1980s. Retribution has become the all-too-acceptable substitute for efforts to rehabilitate delinquent youth.

Juvenile Delinquency

Noncompliant youth—whether subjects for exile, for criminal punishment or juvenile justice—have been in the eye of social and political storms throughout recorded history. If the civilization of a society can be measured by the treatment of its youth, an even more accurate measure may be found in the treatment of its delinquent youth. By this measure, America has won mixed, high and, recently, low marks.

The early Puritans, like their biblical ancestors, decreed harsh punishments for youths who failed to respect their moral teachings. For a time, public officials were appointed to police compliance with religious obligations. A century later, when the labor of poor children was of value to commerce, motives to protect property interests and to provide child care were intermingled. In the early 19th century, Josiah Quincy, after visiting textile mills in New England, pleaded for children put to work at the age of 4. The employers replied that the labor of these children prevented "idleness, rambling, and vicious habits," and also aided competition with the British industry.[1] Similar arguments defeated Federal restrictions on child labor for the next 100 years with the justification that it would invade "the sanctity of the family."[2]

By the mid-19th century, more men and women followed in the footsteps of Josiah Quincy. Individuals, nonsectarian societies and religious organizations developed charitable institutions to care for needy children. Interest in delinquent children came more slowly. Strangely, concern for what happened to delinquents appeared originally from a different source. A small number of correctional officers and voluntary managers of correctional institutions, who observed incarcerated youth, acknowledged their failure to do more than enforce obedience while delinquents were under lock and key (See chapter 3).

In this country, there were also the optimistic beliefs that delinquent children could be rehabilitated, and that injustices to children would be corrected if exposed to the public. It was in this spirit that a small group of settlement-house workers, philanthropists, and a few lawyers presented the idea of a Children's Court as a step toward justice for juveniles. They urged work with youths as more productive than punishment. They rejected labeling or treating youths as adult criminals.

The concept that a Children's Court should be of help to children—whether dependent, neglected, or delinquent—survived for decades. In the 1930s when I began work on the court in New York, the petitions still read "In the Matter of John D." and asked the court to take action in the best interest of the child. In those Depression days, two aspects of city life were far different. Front doors were still left unlocked, and walking in the streets was not limited by fear of strangers. Second, in the midst of widespread misery, the delinquencies of children seemed minor. Truancy, misbehavior at home or in school, staying out late, and small thefts were the grist for delinquency charges. Delinquents were rarely charged with violent acts. There were few deadly weapons around in those days and the use of knives was infrequent. Drug abuse or alcoholism among youth was practically unknown. For the few shocking offenses, such as murder or manslaughter, the Criminal Courts took jurisdiction.

Only two constant differences appeared in those days between neglect and delinquency cases: A majority of the children in neglect cases were under 12 years of age, whereas a majority of the youth charged with delinquency were over 12. The second major difference was determined by whether the complainant was seeking aid or punishment. The physically abused child and the violent, assaultive youth were the exceptions.

It took time to realize that the absence of official labels did not end other pervasive labeling that affected justice to delinquent children. Poverty, class, and race affected which children were brought to court, and how they fared in court. The police were more likely to refer a child to a social agency than to make an arrest if they saw the family as "respectable." Aid from a voluntary agency was more likely than a trial if the family appeared reliable.[3] The education, language, dress, and manners of parents counted for or against their children. Sudden or recent poverty was less subject to stigma than long-term dependency. Like well-dressed beggars, those who wore their poverty best received the most sympathy and help.

The court was expected to finalize earlier labels attached by teachers, social workers, public welfare, and the police. As a rule, neither parents nor the delinquent took exception to the charges set forth in words they often did not understand.

Court procedures did not invite seeing behind the masks worn by delinquent youth. Those arrested or held in detention entered the courtroom through one side door. Parents entered by a different door when called from the waiting room. Usually the child and parent had not seen each other since "the trouble." As delinquents entered the court, they glanced quickly at a parent or looked anxiously for missing parents. Most said nothing. Sad or sullen, expressions changed as the parent looked toward a child or turned away in anger. Only unusual incidents pierced the masks delinquents wore. One boy charged with a theft did not look at his mother as she turned to him. He stood silent and remote before the bench as though he did not see her. Suddenly she swayed and in an instant the boy caught her in his arms and placed her in a chair with tenderness. Then pulling himself together, he returned to stand before the bench as though nothing had happened and as though his mother was not present. His mask was back, but the judge could see behind it to the boy's feelings for his mother that he could not admit.

Parents, too, were silent before the court. But there were wonderful exceptions. One black mother on welfare taught a lesson not to be forgotten. She had been summoned to court when her 10-year-old son was charged with truancy and misbehavior by his school principal. After hearing the testimony of the principal, I asked the mother if she had anything to say. She spoke with dignity in simple words that electrified the courtroom: "This principal sent for me and said I should whip my boy in front of his class or he would not be promoted. I told her if he was smart enough to be promoted with a whipping, he was smart enough to be promoted without one. That's why she brought him and me to court."

This mother had shown the vast difference between the charges alleging delinquency and the world that she and her son enjoyed together. In fairytale fashion, the boy became a well-known author many years later. He had learned to use English in the straight and colorful language of his mother.

Spread of Labeling in Juvenile Justice

Despite the initial efforts to avoid treating children on the basis of labels, juvenile delinquents always held a special and prominent position in the administration of juvenile justice. Each delinquent appeared in his own orbit. Acts and demeanor were all-important. The 12-year-old boy who had stolen a bicycle and the weeping girl of 14, locked out by her parents for violating curfew for the third time, could not be confused. What a child had done and whether he or she looked sorrowful or defiant were both important. The judge had the specific delinquency as a basis for judgment. This was far less complicated and less painful than evaluating a morass of charges in a neglect complaint that required the judge to enter the life of a family. The single or isolated act of delinquency was easier to grasp than the frayed issues that made up family life.

By the late 1930s, a return to labeling was encouraged by probation officers and agency workers who complained that youth were becoming more aggressive each year. At first their complaints sounded like a Greek chorus, intended to secure more funding or lighter caseloads. However, when the country became absorbed in war preparations and more parents went to work, youth were left with less supervision and fewer services. Their problems multiplied and more delinquents were charged with violent acts.

Juvenile Justice in Wartime

The separation of neglected from delinquent children followed swiftly on reports of an alarming rise in delinquency here and in England, beginning in the early days of World War II. Under the pressure of numbers and reports of greater violence, looking at the whole child in terms of his life history and individual problems was displaced. The old belief that "bad" and "good" children, like apples, should not be mixed regained currency. New rules required that child-care agencies should limit their services to either neglected or delinquent children.

Social agencies were quicker to follow these rules than those requiring higher standards of care or an end to racial discrimination. Charters were amended to restrict admission to either neglected or delinquent children. Labeling was given added impetus by the separation of state fiscal responsibility for the residential care of delinquent children, and the continuing fiscal responsibility of localities for the support of neglected children. Each eyed the other, determined not to be burdened unduly. When some judges balked, unwilling to send a child to an institution for delinquents because of some minor delinquency following long-term neglect, both state and city rejected findings of "delinquency due to neglect."[4,5]

Ten-year-old Peter was charged with delinquency for taking some change from his mother's purse. The probation investigation revealed the mother had never wanted him, and had brought him to court as a way of getting him out of the home. Yet, in order to secure a foster home for Peter, it was necessary for the judge to dismiss the delinquency petition and to order a neglect petition based solely on the mother's refusal to visit Peter in detention. Such legalistic mumbo-jumbo occasionally could be performed by a judge, but it bore witness to the foolishness of allowing labels to determine the care of a child.

Services for delinquents diminished, as communities demanded they be safeguarded. Judges felt pressures knowing they would be held responsible if a delinquent released to the community engaged in another delinquent act. Wartime was seen as no time for indulgence to delinquent youth.

Gang warfare, largely controlled in earlier periods, broke out with new ferocity between racial, ethnic, and religious groups of adolescents at the beginning of World War II. The war abroad had its imitators among youth in this country.

Early in the 1940s, white gangs in New York attacked Jewish and black school children. During the war, the Irish Dukes, the Allies, the McGintys, the Hurricanes with some Italian members, attacked Puerto Rican newcomers to the Bronx. Police and priests met with the parents of Irish boys to stop interracial and interreligious conflicts. During this period, the principal of a junior high school in Manhattan reported that 20 teenagers had been shot or stabbed in gang wars during the preceding 20 months, not including assaults that did not require hospitalization.

As burglaries and muggings spread to "the better neighborhoods," it was urged that police should again be equipped with clubs. In court, when a youth was charged with violence, one could sense tension and a drawing away as though the youth carried a communicable disease. Juvenile Courts adopted the words, "violent juveniles" as descriptive of youths who lived in depressed areas of the city. The administrative judge regarded sending such youth, mostly nonwhite, to jail as the only way of controlling "precociously vicious young people"[6] and a majority of the judges agreed. Fear and prejudice reached a peak when a well-known conservative called a riot by black and Puerto Rican youth "the night of the animals."

A New Look at Juvenile Justice in the 1960s

It was not until two decades after the war that the Federal government looked closely at the administration of justice in the United States. In 1967, President Johnson's Commission on Law Enforcement and the Administration of Justice published its report. It included significant criticisms of juvenile justice throughout the country. This report blew more than one whistle.[7]

First, it charged the Juvenile Courts with failure to meet the needs of delinquent youth, while resorting to turnstile punishment and overinstitutionalization. These charges were, however, tempered by recognition that "the dispositional alternatives available, even to the better endowed Juvenile Courts, fall far short of the richness and the relevance to individual needs envisioned by the founders." It found that the Juvenile Courts had not been provided with either the personnel or the facilities to fulfill their mission.

Second, the report warned against the tendency to move from efforts to rehabilitate delinquent youth to the philosophy and practices of retribution, deterrence and incapacitation characteristic of the Criminal court system. Third, the report proposed the development of preventive community services for delinquent and pre-delinquent youth. It contended that with such diversionary service in place, only delinquents presenting manifest dangers to themselves or the community would require Juvenile Court intervention.

The unified design drafted by the Task Force was subjected to selective use. The call for services needed by the Juvenile Court for delinquents went unheeded while attacks against the court became more virulent. One eminent sociologist described the court as an "overpainted frumpish dowager in whose company only a few former friends wanted to be seen."[8] The warning against criminalization went unheeded. Only the proposal for diversion took hold for a time. It appealed to the intuitive good will of Americans, satisfied the anti-interventionist mood of the 1970s, and seemed to promise care of youths at less cost.

In July 1974, Congress responded officially to the call for diversionary services by enacting the Juvenile Justice Delinquency and Prevention Act. Its stated purpose was to reduce and to prevent juvenile delinquency. It declared juvenile delinquency a threat to the national welfare, the cause of enormous cost, and a waste of potential human resources. Congress established the Law Enforcement Assistance Administration (LEAA) within the Department of Justice as a corrective vehicle, with the expectation that Youth Service bureaus, supported by public funds, would coordinate local services. But Service Bureaus could not coordinate what did not exist. Few provided shelters, residential care, or other direct services for youths.

LEAA was authorized to subsidize community preventive services and to monitor the separation of noncriminal from criminal youth. Early optimistic reports from LEAA recounted an increase in smaller, more open local facilities and new opportunities for volunteers to work in local programs up to 1976.[9] Evaluations of these programs became scarce. By 1979, the decrease in Federal funding was underway and reduced initial hopes. LEAA listed a sheriff's camping program, a school coordinator for 1 year, and a beautification program for 20 minority teenagers, all located in one town in Arizona and one town in South Carolina, as examples of model programs.[10]

Advocates for preventive services were disillusioned when they saw the focus of diversion shifted to crisis assistance with little aid for habitual truants, persistent runaways, and youths engaged in serious delinquency. They feared that instead of narrowing governmental intervention, the new programs were widening the net for juveniles who would not have been subjected to the Juvenile Court under former procedures.[11] These fears were confirmed in a study by Arthur Little in 1977.[12]

The Little study reported the absence of a clear definition for status offenders; the short supply of rehabilitative services; the absence of mental health services; discriminatory practices; and the failure to monitor deinstitutionalization as required by law. It also pointed to the lack of opportunities for job development and independent living for youths. In each of 10 states studied, the traditional fragmentation of services had continued.

An expert from Norway, who visited California diversionary projects (listed as exemplary by LEAA), noted they did not deal with delinquent youths from the lower classes. Speaking of these projects as a "velvet cloak," she wrote, "They take children from middle class families and neglect the lower class."

Violent Juveniles

Until recently, violence against children in their homes was not recognized. The deaths of small children were described as failures to thrive and parents were not charged with abuse. At the other end of the spectrum, small children who killed were left subject to Criminal Court action and were sent away to correctional institutions or state hospitals, often for life. Why a child had killed, what happened to such a child, and whether he or she remained dangerous to others was not questioned as long as the child was safely put away.

In 1935, Dr. Lauretta Bender, an exceptional child psychiatrist, began a 25-year study of children who had committed homicides. Her final report stated that not one child kept within the Juvenile Court system had recidivated, but that those transferred to the Criminal Courts had been injured by delays in diagnosis and lack of treatment for mental disabilities. In Quebec, a study reported that of 48 adolescents found guilty of homicide, the only one who had recidivated had been transferred for trial to the Criminal Court.[13] Such findings did not affect demands for Criminal Court action as the answer for controlling violent children or youth.

Judges and social agencies acted with caution and fear. During all my years on the bench, I recall only four young children who had killed and who were accepted for residential care and treatment. They were all accepted by Hawthorne, an agency of the Jewish Board of Guardians, between 1943 and 1952. Years later, when I was able to read their records, I learned that each one had made a "good" or "fairly good" adjustment in the community with no further violent incidents.[14]

These histories were far different from that of another boy, Allen, brought to the Juvenile Court for petty stealing when he was only 7. Both his father and a kindly stepfather had died. His mother found Allen a burden. He truanted, wandered the streets, and stole. No agency would accept him because he had "no family" with whom the agencies felt they could work. The state hospital reported Allen as "affection-starved, guarded, and depressed." Still, there was no place for Allen except the State Training School for delinquents. While on parole at 17, this unloved adolescent was involved in a fatal hold-up and was convicted of murder. Sentenced to Attica, he was killed in the 1970 riot before his 20th year. Allen had been made to feel superfluous since childhood. Like those persons described by Hannah Arendt in *Origins of Totalitarianism*, Allen was the "outsider" who turned to the use of violence.

In large cities, many unemployed youth had become alien outsiders. Their wrong doings were not recognized as a symptom of chronic community or subcommunity disease, which spelled risks of violence.

From Victims of Violence to Violent Juveniles

There is nothing new in our violence, only in sudden awareness of it.[15]

Violence toward children and youth has been expressed in endless ways in the history of this country. Deeply rooted in many places, it has been resistant to control. Indifference and inaction in the face of violence to children was hardest to identify when it occurred within the family. It was also difficult to uncover or to challenge when practiced by social institutions. Orders by courts for jailing and incarceration of youth made their suffering invisible. In some periods, violence against youth was disguised in fancy trappings. One thoughtful critic of aversion therapy described it as "the modern equivalent of a turn of the rack, save that in this instance the jailor inflicts this pain in the same breath with which he heralds the regenerative efforts of treatment."[16]

In 1969, Richard Hofstadter wrote that domestic violence was more a part of American history than a tradition of the country. Yet, in his review of the 19th century urban riots, he described the racial and religious prejudices that set the patterns for many episodes of cruelty. In his words, "Too often the contents of the melting pot did not melt, or when they did it was only under fire."[17] The melting of prejudice against minority groups proved an unending task for juvenile justice.

As I look back to the war and postwar period, I find a stubborn reluctance on my part to join in the hue and cry against youth engaged in violent acts. Those who were leading the demands for harsh punishment and longer incarceration had never shown concern about violence against youth, the indifference to their needs or the prejudices that controlled the lives of ghetto youth. In addition, they vaunted an "I told you so" attitude as they pointed contemptuously to violent juveniles. I could refuse to join the pack but I had to face facts as they confronted the court.

From the onset of war, even before the United States had entered it, more juveniles were arrested and charged with violent offenses. The charges were more serious. Assaults against strangers, muggings with weapons, burglaries involving assaults on those robbed, the use and sale of drugs descended on a court unused to such youthful violence except on rare occasions. The behavior of delinquent youths in court had also changed. They appeared more callous, more indifferent about what they had done and about what the court could do to them. In court, a sense of hopelessness in dealing with these youths added one more stumbling block to trying.

Part of the increase in violent offenses could be explained by the diversion of minor delinquencies to other agencies, but the world had become a dangerous planet, and youth increasingly played a part in its dangers. The Juvenile Court was singled out as the place to get rid of dangerous or potentially dangerous youth. Incapacitation was the demand of fearful communities. Judges, with reduced discretion to evaluate individual youths were expected to act only on the delinquent acts. This distanced them from youth in one more way. The judges became instruments for the imposition of community vengeance. The Juvenile Court was increasingly reduced to a way station for the imposing of fixed and longer sentences directly or by transfer to the Criminal Court.

Attacks on violent juveniles continued to avoid underlying causes giving rise to violence in this country. Those in power did not choose to confront the reality that "ours is a gun culture."[18] In 1965 an Opinion Research Poll reported that 34% of whites and 24% of blacks all acknowledged owning guns. Our homicide gun rate remained the highest of that in any advanced nation. Our country and our youth paid a heavy price for the victories of the gun lobby in Washington.

In 1986, the rising pattern of gang activity and of violence was reported to have taken hold in many states across the country. Incidents of manslaughter and murder were reported in Jackson, Denver, Minneapolis, Baton Rouge, Tulsa, Chatanooga, and Atlanta. The large cities were reported to be most infected, with Chicago having 135 gangs and 1,300 hard-core gang members involved in a broad range of criminal activities. New York was at the low end, with 66 gangs and 2,000 members reported by the police, compared with a far higher number a decade earlier.

According to police and gang experts, unemployment, boredom, and alienation among black youths and other minority groups had bred an environment ripe for gang development.[19]

Retribution and incapacitation of delinquent youth had been made reputable, if not mandatory. Even some liberals had swallowed the concept of retribution as the solution when disguised as "just deserts," not seeing it as a reversion to vengeance. In New York, as elsewhere, mandatory and longer sentences together with sending more youths back to the Criminal Courts had become the order of the day by the mid-1970s.[20]

Retribution and Recriminalization of Youth

In the 1970s, waivers of seriously delinquent youths to the Criminal courts was the favored substitute for individualized justice in almost every state. Waivers were authorized at younger and younger ages. They reduced pressure for providing appropriate services through the Juvenile Court. No one kept book on youths, who were made to disappear temporarily into the Criminal Court system and prisons. And, no one kept track of what happened on their return to the community.

The first Supreme Court decision involving waiver to the Criminal court held that a youth was entitled to procedural due process (*Kent*). In a later case, the court held that waiver did not justify subjecting a youth to double jeopardy.[21] However, the court also stated in 1975 that all juveniles could not benefit from the Juvenile Court, and that a procedure for transfer to an adult court should be made available. No standards were set for the services that the adult court must provide.

Waiver legislation swept the country. States differed as to the age of a youth that could trigger its use. A majority authorized use for serious offenses at 14 years of age, with some states limiting its use to youths of 16 or older, whereas others moved down to 13 and even younger ages. In many states the authority to seek waiver was given to prosecuting attorneys. Some statutes required the Juvenile Court judge to consider age, the previous record of a child, the likelihood of rehabilitation, and the facilities available to the Juvenile Court before resorting to the use of waiver. Other statutes required that the judge be satisfied that it was not in the interest of the juvenile to send him or her to any facilities available to the Juvenile Court. None required that the Juvenile Court find that the Criminal Court could or would provide facilities preferable to those available to the Juvenile Court.

Three arguments were presented in favor of returning children to the Criminal courts. First, by providing a "get tough" approach, the community would receive or feel it was receiving greater protection. Second, waiver legislation moved from the "hopeless" goal of rehabilitation to retribution and "just deserts" for youth. Finally, this procedure added no additional direct costs to state budgets. After the IJA-ABA agreed to approve waivers for 15-year-olds, its director described waiver as the "last resort of a just society."

New York was one of the very few states to resist waiving youths to the Criminal Courts. When the demands that juveniles be locked up became more vociferous, Governor Carey did what bombarded governors often do. He appointed a commission to study the subject under the chairmanship of Dr. Kevin Cahill, his close friend and Commissioner of Health. The commission included a motley crew of politicians, public figures, a few judges, and a few civil libertarians. A subcommittee was appointed to deal with the subject of juvenile violence. That subcommitte collected studies, interviewed experts, and became satisfied that it was not possible to predict which delinquent youths would be violent in the future. When the legislators insisted on more incarceration based on predictions, Dr. Cahill persuaded the Governor not to yield and a compromise was reached in 1976.

However, the temper of the times demanded more, and in 1978 a law that went beyond waivers was enacted. This "Juvenile Offender Law" directed the police to take youths aged 14 and 15 charged with the most serious offenses (murder, kidnapping, arson, assault, rape, sodomy, burglary, robbery of certain degrees) directly to the Criminal Courts and included 13-year-olds charged with murder. The results presented an ugly caricature of justice for youth.

Reviewing "The Experiment that Failed," the Citizens' Committee for Children of New York, Inc. reported on the months that youths were held in detention or jail awaiting trials, the return of many youths to the Family Court (39.4%), and the limited number of prosecutions successfully completed. The promise of swift, effective punishment of youths who committed felonies proved to be a mirage.

This independent stand of the Citizens' Committee for Children recalls its founding 40 years ago. A few people working with children had been searching individually to find people in and outside government, sensitive to the problems of children. We felt the time had come to work together, so we met late one afternoon in the small garden of my home. The group included Dr. Neva Deardorff, a pioneer researcher; Larry Frank, a social philosopher; Alice Kelliher and Roma Gans, distinguished educators; Dr. Marion E. Kenworthy and Dr. Viola W. Bernard, both psychiatrists and teachers at Columbia University; Dr. Leona Baumgartner, Commissioner of Public Health; Adele R. Levy, civic leader in many social causes; my husband, and myself.

As we talked, we agreed there was need for an independent voluntary agency, where men and women could work together as individuals, rather than as representatives of organizations, of political groups, or of vested interests. Shad Polier offered his services as counsel and Adele Levy provided the funds needed to get the work going. Charlotte Carr became the first director. She gave great leadership for a decade and was followed by Dr. Trude Lash, who did much to strengthen the work of the committee. Today it is led by Bernard C. Fisher, an expert in the child welfare field who is deeply committed to increased community participation by experts and lay volunteers.

The Citizens' Committee invited and secured the cooperation of outstanding experts in health, education, social welfare, and juvenile justice. Everyone worked as a volunteer on committees appointed over the years, with the support of a small professional staff. Studies, investigations, and published reports became effective tools for educating the public and for placing greater responsibility on public and voluntary agencies. The Committee has not always been popular, but its work has gained a wide hearing and great respect.

Underlying Threats to Juvenile Justice

Two major threats had existed and grown before World War II. The ongoing use of jails and prisons to hold youth of Juvenile Court age was a clear and specific violation of law never corrected by the states or Federal government. The second threat was far more insidious, widespread, and difficult to confront. It arose from the general distancing in this country of youth who needed aid from both government and individuals who would provide aid when it was needed.

Jails and Prisons for Children

Removal of youths from adult jails and prisons had been one of the first goals of the Children's Court movement and was widely accepted by state legislators creating the Juvenile Courts. Yet, the incarceration of children in institutions holding adult criminals was flagrant, abetted by a conspiracy of silence. Seeing no evil, governmental agencies avoided speaking of it.

In 1952, I inquired about the use of jails for children from the Federal Children's Bureau. The response read: "Unfortunately we have no figures. It has been estimated that anywhere from 50,000 to 100,000 children are detained in jail each year."[22] State and local agencies, including the Juvenile Courts, that placed delinquents, played their part in the same blind man's bluff. They did not visit the jails to which they sent children. Some few judges also chose to send children to jail to shock them into better behavior. Welfare departments even used jails to house retarded and neglected children when hard pressed for space.

Reports of beatings and torture of youths by adult criminals and of suicides by adolescents held in jail forced occasional state investigations. Renewed opposition to the use of jails for children and youth finally led to Federal legislation. However, once again the Federal Juvenile Justice and Delinquency Act in 1974 showed no sense of urgency. It provided for the withdrawal of Federal funds to states only if they did not remove all juveniles from adult jails and lock-ups by 1988. Twelve of the 14 years allowed had passed by 1986, but Federal experts stated that 240,000 youths would be held in jails in 1986.[23] It was reported that only 27 of the 50 states were "moving strongly" toward compliance with the Federal prohibition against jail for juveniles.

The failure to end the imprisonment of juveniles with adults was symptomatic of the endless discrepancies between principles enunciated and actual practices affecting juvenile delinquents, when justice and institutional habits were at odds. On visits to detention homes and jails in the early 1970s, I found shameful conditions. They had become shabby, deteriorated catch-alls for youths, and had few programs for education or work. Even the few new jails, although spic and span, were empty holding places.

Distancing Delinquent Youth

Justice Brandeis, long interested in the Juvenile Court, told me one day of a far away land where those who decreed human sacrifice never touched their victims. The executioners were given instruments of death with long handles, so that they, too, would be distanced from the victims. He said no more, but that tale came to mind many times as I watched governmental officials—legislators, administrators, and judges distance themselves from delinquent youth.

In the early days when voluntary agencies accepted more delinquents, they limited their responsibility to work with the child and rarely worked with the families. That was left to the Welfare Departments. This separated family members from children in placement. Children were lonely and caring family members were ignored or distanced.

Timothy and his grandmother came before me for review of his placement. The agency that had had custody for 8 of his 11 years asked for continuing placement. Timothy began to sob and his grandmother put a loving arm around him. The agency worker explained, in a brisk manner, that return to the grandmother had been disapproved because Timothy's addicted mother resided there. Then the grandmother spoke up. She had not seen the mother during the past 5 years, and two of Timothy's sisters who had been released to her for care by another agency were doing well. On questioning by the court, the agency worker admitted that he had never visited the grandmother's home, but explained that the records showed the mother had once given the grandmother's address as her own. Whether because of embarrassment or change of viewpoint, he immediately approved Timothy's discharge to the grandmother.

Within the Juvenile Court there was no single villain or point of departure for the distancing of delinquents. Juvenile justice was slowly deformed as it separated and was separated from both delinquent and neglected youth. Direct contact with delinquent youth was short circuited as youths were transferred to state authorities for placement. Judges were relieved of responsibility for deciding whether open, moderate, or secure facilities were appropriate in individual cases, and they were excluded from seeing or gauging the consequences of state decisions. Distancing of neglected children moved along in similar fashion, as they were siphoned off to the Welfare Departments for decisions on placement. Even the court requirement that it be notified if placement were not secured within a reasonable period, went largely ignored and fell into disuse.

When dispositions were removed from court responsibility, delinquent and neglected children were made more vulnerable to the political climate of each period. That climate affected whether delinquents were more or less likely to be sent to secure facilities. It affected the methods used for shuffling neglected children into existing cubbyholes. Often unseen, these children were placed on the basis of tags, showing only age, sex, and religion.

Youth with special problems, such as mental retardation or emotional disturbances, fell into a no man's land. So, too, did youth with serious physical handicaps. Voluntary agencies did not accept them and many states were not ready to develop new facilities. A response came from those who were ever ready to provide services for profit, and youths were sent to far away places under agreements by the states to pay for them under individual contracts. This new form of banishment left youths unvisited and unsupervised in places distant from their homes. It was not until the 1970s that the resulting injuries to youths were challenged by public exposure and court actions.

It was not only placement procedures that distanced youth from securing the aid they needed. The limited concern of professionals in the problems of youth played an important role. A study by one psychiatrist of children charged with homicide, showed that each had had a previous history of serious injuries to the central nervous system but had never received adequate medical attention.[24] By the 1970s, when the New York Juvenile Court judges were asked to report on all cases they had held for over 60 days before entering dispositions, few could answer. They did not know, and such accountings were not kept. Even the small research unit in the court had been abolished for reasons of economy.

Judges at every judicial level accepted distancing delinquent youth by preference, convenience, or because of "new rules." In the Juvenile Court, many judges placed greater emphasis on higher benches and the wearing of robes as essential to receiving respect. They had forgotten the lesson of Judge Baker of Boston who, a half century ago, stepped down from his bench in order to sit on a level with the youths brought in before him. Less sure of their role, they reached for the trappings of office. When I visited Cook County, where the Juvenile Court originated, the low regard in which it was held was underlined by the practice of assigning its judgeship as a booby prize to the judge who received the lowest vote in the previous election.

Self-distancing from youths likewise appeared in Supreme Court decisions. It was epitomized in the opinion of Justice Rehnquist, approving preventive detention for youth prior to trial. He wrote that "juveniles unlike adults, were always in some form of custody."[25] He was apparently oblivious of or indifferent to the thousands of homeless youths across the country.

Reformers in the 1970s, intent on minimizing intervention by the Juvenile Courts, also distanced the juvenile delinquent. They accepted harsh punishments and longer incarceration without services in return for the promise of removing the noncriminal or status offenders from court jurisdiction. Lesser interest in "true delinquents" allowed violation of civil liberties and civil rights. School records and prior offenses were opened to adult courts, employers, and credit unions. The Federal government required information on youth admitted to state drug programs as a condition for Federal funding. Only Massachusetts refused to yield to this violation of privacy. One thoughtful Juvenile Court judge noted that in 7 years on the bench, only two middle-class youths had been presented as "dangerous youths."[26] "Criminal subculture" had become the code words applied to distinguish and distance the world of poor and black delinquents.

Distancing delinquent youth spread a self-comforting anesthesia to everyone except youths charged with offenses. It curtailed off these youths from concern and from sight. In Minnesota, when an Appellate Court ordered a judicial investigation of waivers of youth to the Criminal Courts, what happened was laid bare for the first time. The investigating judge reported that there were no services for children over 13 years of age brought before either the juvenile or adult courts. He described youths relegated to rows of stone and steel cages " without assurance of protection from crime-prone, depraved young adults."[27] Minnesota was not unique. Vacant parts of old prisons and state hospitals had become the newest and cheapest way of restraining serious delinquents in many states.

Self-righteousness accompanied the doing of less for delinquent youths supported by the theory that nothing worked. In 1981, the Reagan Task Force on Violent Crimes raised the white flag as a defense for doing less with some hedging: "We are not convinced that a government, by the invention of new programs or the management of existing institutions, can by itself recreate those familial and neighborhood conditions, those social opportunities, and those personal values that in all likelihood are the prerequisites of tranquil communities."[28]

This prescription for further distancing of delinquent youth was a late model. It did not refer to the findings of the 1967 Federal commission that efforts to rehabilitate youth had been minuscule. It did not refer to the 1979 National Academy of Science report that questioned the conclusion that nothing had worked and asked what had been given a fair chance. Rather, it gave support to the summary by Judge David Bazelon of the changing response of America to juvenile delinquency. He wrote that the corrective areas of rehabilitation gave way to deterrence, now being replaced by incapacitation, a fancy word for "lock the bastards up."[29]

Chapter 3
The Drive for Punishment: Violence Against Youth

What is common to all punishments is the emphatic and direct humbling of the noncompliant will.[1]

Of the many definitions of punishment, this may well be the most accurate. In juvenile justice, police, social agencies, and judges have all been influenced by whether a youth appeared contrite. Demands for humbling survived changing theories and practices of rehabilitation, deterrence, behavior modification[2] and, now, for "just deserts."[3] Apparent humility has been a price demanded from those who seek charity. In depression days, parents who could not provide food or clothing, thanked judges for finding them "neglectful" so that their children could be placed in orphanages. When judges visited institutions, teachers clapped their hands to have children stand at attention and sing songs of gratitude. In court, a look or gesture of disgust by a probation officer, social worker, or judge were tools for humbling a child or parent.

How to measure punishment, however, is rarely presented in such forthright words as those of Jeremy Bentham: "If you hate much, punish much, if you hate little, punish little, punish as you hate."[4]

The vogue in punishments provide candid photographs and in-depth portraits of periodic societal values. Emile Durkheim wrote, 100 years after Bentham, that the average reaction to acts that offended the collective sentiments of a community determined whether they would be treated as crimes or moral faults.[5] Nowhere is it more apparent than in the punishments of deviant youth. Since the 1960s, when youthful defiance of societal mores spread to wider economic and social classes, much of such conduct was reduced from delinquency to a new category: "youths in need of supervision." In this same period, in accordance with the theories of Bentham and Durkheim, the sale or use of narcotics was made a criminal offense while truancy, late hours, and promiscuity were reduced to moral faults. It took the civil rights movement to erase miscegenation as a criminal offense.

Violence Against Youth

Violence practiced against juvenile offenders has had a long, varied and recurrent history in all countries. Granting full pardons to the very young was common practice in England before the 14th century. The age of nonresponsibility was raised to 13 and 14 in 1338; and in the 16th century, 15 was urged as the appropriate age of criminal responsibility.[6] But, by the 18th century, brutal and capital punishments were restored. In 1835, a 9-year-old was executed in England for stealing a small quantity of printer's ink through a broken window.

Within fewer centuries and in shorter cycles, violent punishment of youth and opposition to its use succeeded one another in this country. In pre-colonial days, capital punishment was prescribed for 16 offenses, including striking a parent, although no record has been found of its application. In the mid-19th century, the superintendent of the Chicago Reform School warned, "Remove a boy from the old haunts of crime, shut him out from the world, shut him up by himself, let him march with locked step, wheel him to the right, wheel him to the left with the most precise military discipline. Yet, know that when your maneuvers are through you are ignorant of the mind and soul of the tractable machine."

In 1853, the volunteer managers of the New York Reformatory decried the deadly boredom of youth locked up without employment, who were "doomed to moral destitution." Two other observations in that early period foreshadowed persistent problems. The words "proportionate punishment," revived in the 1970s, were invoked to modify both "too rigorous punishment" and "the danger of impunity from punishment." At the same time, it was noted that "every thing seems to be calculated to avoid unnecessary expense."[7]

From early in the 19th century, reformers in this country urged that children should be separated from adults convicted of crimes. In New York, the House of Refuge was established in 1835 by private philanthropists.

However the circuit court judges retained the power to decide which youths should be referred, and the House of Refuge was given the final decision as to which youths it would accept. It was only in 1894 that New York amended its laws to allow judges to try children under 14 years of age as misdemeanants, unless charged with a capital offense. Other amendments followed and in 1909, the term *juvenile delinquent* replaced *criminal offender* for children under 16 years of age, unless the offense charged was punishable by death or life imprisonment.

In Illinois, the history was different. A father challenged the commitment of his son to a reformatory in 1870. The court, finding that his boy's offense was not criminal, granted a writ of habeas corpus stating that his confinement was evidently taken "under the general grant of power to arrest and confine for misfortune."[8] The judge went further, adding, "It is claimed that the law is administered for the moral welfare and intellectual improvement of the minor and the good of society. From the record before us, we know nothing of the management." Such perspicacity and skepticism about the management of institutions were rarely expressed by judges in either juvenile or adult courts then or in the present.

Among all the states, Massachusetts was first to create a public state-run institution for juvenile delinquents in the 19th century. This followed a report on 97 children, aged 6 to 16, who had been sentenced to the House of Corrections. The new institution was given authority to determine the length of commitment. Theodore Lyman, a benefactor of this institution, expressed concern about what would happen to these youth as long as citizens showed interest in youths only on ceremonial occasions.

Ironically, during the late 1960s, it was in Massachusetts that the reform institution of an earlier era became the symbol of violence used against children and of all that had gone wrong in the institutional care of delinquents. When Jerome Miller was appointed Commissioner of the Massachusetts Department of Youth Services in 1969, he found the Lyman School cruel, desolate and manned by a punitive staff resistant to all change. Frustrated by their noncooperation, Miller closed most of the training schools and contracted with voluntary agencies for service in the communities.

This approach raised intense controversy. Civil service staff in the established institutions were defensive and fearful of losing their jobs. Voluntary agencies, although welcoming greater financial support from the state, insisted on their traditional right to choose whom they would serve, and to practice racial discrimination.[9] When youth were placed in foster care in local communities, they were not welcomed as neighbors. Judges complained of the lack of adequate facilities for serious delinquents and claimed this made it necessary to transfer more youths to the Criminal Courts. Miller was also criticized for poor administration and high costs. Despite all criticism and the forced departure of Miller from his position, important progress had been made toward a decrease in the number of children subjected to institutional violence. At the same time, the continuing, if not growing, use of secure detention and referrals to the Criminal Courts went on.

There were few in institutional staff positions to defend youth against institutional abuse. But, one evening in 1938, after a day in court, a gifted young psychiatrist told me of his anguish over the punishment meted out at the State Training School. He spoke of the use of fear as the favored instrument for securing compliance from boys 12 to 16 years of age. A few staff members had devised their own peculiar ways of terrorizing boys who misbehaved. One ducked boys through a hole in the ice when they became sexually aroused. Another marched black boys who feared snakes through a marsh at night. A third forced boys who wet their beds to lick the floors in front of other boys. These punishments were sanctioned by an administrator who had organized rock-pile duty that required boys to load and unload rocks on the double under watchful supervisors. The names of boys to be punished were posted regularly on bulletin boards to add to their fear and humiliation.

The following Saturday, a colleague and I used our statutory authority to make an unannounced visit to the school. We were met by a surprised administrator. After a few formal exchanges, we asked to visit the cottages. There we saw the bulletin board listing the boys who were to be punished, and we saw boys on their knees, polishing immaculate floors. Their sullen silence hung heavy and they did not even look up to see who had come in. At one cottage the administrator shouted to a boy to stand up saying, "Tom, I want these judges to see the meanest black man in captivity." Eventually, after our report of what we had seen, this administrator was forced to resign. The new administrator asked the psychiatrist and a social worker to end the reign of terror enforced by his precedessor.

In contrast to the widespread acceptance of punishment as the only effective method of treating delinquent youth, Dr. George Gardner, director of the Judge Baker Guidance Clinic in Boston, spoke of his years of work with delinquent boys and girls. He found that most frequently their personality defects resulted from their seeing the external world as hostile and from never having felt loved or wanted. To illustrate his point, he told of an adolescent who described a human being as "a cobra who swang into position to strike when another animal (meaning himself) came near."[10]

Although various steps were taken to challenge the cruelty within state institutions in the 1970s, they failed to counter recurrent demands for more corporal punishment. The use of physical punishment in homes, schools and institutions was widely condoned and approved. When chairing an investigation in 1974 of the physical abuse of children in a public school, I heard many parents and teachers express approval of corporal punishment as a necessary aid to improving attendance, learning, and behavior.[11] State Boards with responsibility for supervising institutions had long shied away from ending corporal punishment, questioning their power to do so.[12] It is only recently that a few social critics have regarded the extensive use of physical punishment of children in the United States as a major contributory factor in subsequent child abuse of the next generation.[13]

The Pendulum Swings Again in the 1980s

On the national scene as well as in many states, a battle cry was raised against "violent juveniles." The achievements of the late 1960s and early 1970s in securing more humane treatment of incarcerated youth were undermined by the new focus on drug users and runaways, and the decreased Federal funding for community services. Hostility toward violent youths was reflected in indifference to what happened to them once "put away." Exaggerated reports of increased violent offenses by youths continued despite figures showing that only 1% of the arrests for violent offenses in 1978 were by youth under 16 years of age. Pressures on legislatures to waive younger and younger delinquents to the Criminal Courts for trial and punishment grew, and the legislatures responded to these pressures.

Noncriminal Offenders

By the mid-1970s, the Federal government and 22 states had followed the New York model of establishing separate labels and punishments for youths based on whether or not they were charged with criminal offenses. The new labels for noncriminal offenders, "Persons In Need of Super-

vision," "Juveniles In Need of Supervision," or "Minors In Need of Supervision" were widely adopted. New labels were supported by public law advocates who saw themselves as "freedom fighters" against the coercion
employed by the Juvenile Courts. Anything a court did was described as
"coercive." These reformers unwittingly pandered to the hate and fear of
"violent juveniles," while they concentrated on bargaining to reduce punishment for juveniles whose behavior evoked less community fear or anger.
An experienced judge called this process a "gung-ho" approach to juvenile
delinquency.

State courts followed the legislative requirements for separating those
labeled delinquent from youths defined as in need of supervision. After a
boy, released from a State Training School by an Appellate Court, because
he had been found to be a Person In Need of Supervision (PINS), stabbed
and killed another boy, the Appellate Court (in a subsequent case) expressed
concern only for those labeled as PINS. It stated that the statutory requirement for separation directed that a PINS youth should not be confined in a
prison atmosphere along with juveniles committed for criminal acts: "Our
role should be to assure the presence of bona fide treatment programs." No
such concern was expressed for delinquents. By 1975, 36 states had enacted
laws waiving youth to the Criminal Courts, and others were soon to follow.

Punishing Parents

Anger against delinquents spilled over periodically into drives to
punish their parents, with little regard for what parents had done or were
able to do to prevent delinquency. In 1944, the President's Committee for
the Prevention of Juvenile Delinquency wrote to me asking whether I and
my fellow judges were "enforcing the penal law against parents who failed
to exercise reasonable diligence" in the control of their children.[14] In 1947,
public clamor demanded punishment of the mother of a 14-year-old boy
who had shot a man. The boy had been committed to the State Training
School until he became 21, but the media and the police demanded more
punishment. The mother was charged with contributing to the boy's delinquency by not keeping a proper home. Without counsel, she was convicted
and sentenced to State Prison. It took Albert Deutsch, a great investigative
reporter for the newspaper *P.M.*, to discover that the mother had had no

counsel, had not understood the charges, and that the prison had found her so mentally ill that she had been transferred to a state hospital.[15]

The pursuit of parents reached a different and ludicrous level in 1953 when Robert Moses, the great New York City Parks Commissioner, proposed a law to fine or imprison the parents of children who committed vandalism in his beloved parks.[16] When told that such a law would prevent the use of parks by children whose parents could not accompany them, the Commissioner reportedly replied that in such cases a governess should be made responsible.[17]

Within the Juvenile Courts, fines or imprisonment were imposed by law on parents when their children truanted. When one little girl was charged with school truancy, a sad-looking father explained that when he went to work, his wife piled garbage in front of the door to keep evil spirits away and that the child could not get out and go to school. When asked whether he would like the court to help in getting medical care for his wife, he answered in amazement, "Could you?"

The "punish the parents" doctrine spread periodically with few questions as to the results. When one thoughtful judge wrote to the Toledo, Ohio court that had been active in punishing parents for over a decade (1937 to 1947) for its results, the Toledo Court acknowledged that its program had failed to reduce delinquency or the number of parents contributing to it. The answer added that the chief result had been to give satisfaction to nondelinquent parents. Still, the pursuit went on, as exemplified in a 1974 editorial of the *New York Daily News* titled, "Try Soaking the Parents."

Freedom and Punishment in the 1970s

Advocacy to reduce governmental intervention in the lives of families was loudly voiced in Washington, in academia and by the reformers in the 1970s. At the same time, general demands for crime control molded new punishments. The contradictory movements ran on tracks that remained apart.

In "progressive California," old prejudices and new punishments at the state and local levels appeared almost simultaneously. In the name of law and order, a prominent police chief instituted "Operation TRASH," an acronym for Total Resource Attack on Southwest Hoodlums. Black youths who lived in this area were rounded up on flimsy evidence and crowded into a juvenile detention center where they were left to sleep on the floor.

This occurred in the 1970s even as the pseudoscience of "behavior modification" was promoted as a reform measure. In Whittier, California, I visited a secure institution that housed 400 juveniles. It based discharges on a point system. When a boy did not behave, he was confined to a cell in a disciplinary cottage. No human contact was allowed in what the staff proudly described as a "barren and sterile" environment, until the boy showed signs of contrition and readiness to conform. Then he was returned step-by-step to the world of other human beings in accordance with the institutional measurements of "successful behavior modification." No one discussed how such isolation affected different boys, or whether it increased their sense of helplessness or resentment of all authority.

In this same period of the 1970s, the Youth Authority of California, long regarded as a model for constructive aid to youth, was brought under the control of the Departments of Corrections, and the Youth Service bureau was placed under the authority of the police. Subsidies to support preventive services by probation were diminished. Federal funds from the Law Enforcement Assistance Administration (LEAA) were diverted from preventive service to increase police hardware and to support the building of more secure institutions.

There was heated controversy between those who espoused greater freedom from adults who had "mucked up youth long enough," and those demanding harsher punishment for delinquents. Those favoring more recriminalization of delinquent youths won the battle. This was not peculiar to California. Conflicting patterns of thought and action in many places combined opposition to Juvenile Court intervention and advocacy for more police with longer incarceration of youthful offenders.

Recriminalization of Children and Youth

The gravity with which an offense was viewed and the age of a child had once more been made major criteria for determining punishment. Fingerprinting was authorized for children as young as 11.[18] Added punishments included the restriction of family visits although long regarded as most helpful to rehabilitation. In 1978, the Federal Omnibus Crime Bill authorized new funds for prisons and the criminal justice system but none for services to either adult or juvenile offenders. The major "concession" to juvenile justice was to rename the Crime Control Bill, "The Justice Model." This euphemism was used to justify concentrating on a small number of serious offenders, while ignoring the large number of needy youths not regarded as "dangerous."

Retreads of old arguments about the punishment of youth have been constant for at least 1,000 years. The discourse between an unnamed abbot and Saint Anselm in 1100 A.D. shows how little society has progressed in its use of punishment through the centuries.

The abbot asked:
"What, pray, can we do with them? They are perverse and incorrigible; day and night we cease not to chastise them, yet they grow daily worse and worse."

Anselm marvelled and said:
"Ye cease not to beat them? And when they are grown to manhood, of what sort are they then?"

The abbot said:
"They are dull and brutish."

Then said Anselm:
"Tell me, I prithee, if thou shouldst plant a sapling in thy garden and presently shut it on all sides so that it could nowhere extend its branches; when thou hast liberated it after many years, what manner of tree would come forth? Would it not be wholly unprofitable, with gnarled and tangled branches? And whose fault would it be but thine own, who has closed it in beyond all reason. Thus without doubt do ye with your children...ye hem them in every side with terrors, threats and stripes...[so] that they put forth a tangle of evil thoughts like thorns...Hence it cometh to pass that, perceiving in you no love for themselves, no pity, no kindness, no gentleness, they are unable henceforth to trust in your goodness...."[19]

Chapter 4
Neglected and Abused Children

This particular child was fixed, as a fly is fixed in glue, she could not move; she was held in the original position of "the neglected one," of the one who had been left or the one who could not find a way to give, who was thus cut off, as it were.[1]

Judges do not sense such exquisite pain. Belief in the resiliency of children prevents seeing what happens to the less resilient. Only cases of gross neglect are presented for court action.

Restrictions on Aid to Poor Children

The Juvenile Court was heir to many restrictions placed on aid to the indigent. During the 1890s when the Juvenile Court movement was a-borning in Illinois, a New York court held, "It is no part of the duty of the overseers [of the poor] to search out [the pauper].... He is not the chooser of the place and manner of his support, and must take what is to be had."[2] In keeping with this viewpoint, children of the poor were moved through a series of public and private institutions by those who had the power to dispose of their lives, and who assumed they knew what it was best to do.

Arbitrary disposal of poor children flowed from disapproval and condemnation of their parents. In the 19th century, Charles Loring Brace was acclaimed for taking children from "haunts of poverty, drudgery and vice inflicted by immigrant parents." No sympathy was shown for the necessities or feelings of their parents. The children were placed in the homes of midwest farmers who offered keep in return for unpaid labor. What happened to these children and their parents is not known. But a contemporary description of their auctioning describes the harsh realities of this well-intentioned reform.

> The children ... were taken directly from the train to the court- house, where a large crowd gathered.... Then, if the child gave assent, the bargain was concluded on the spot. It was a pathetic sight ... to see those children and young people, weary, travel- stained, confused ... peering into those strange faces, and trying to choose wisely for themselves.[3]

Deep into the 20th century little heed was paid to indigent parents as their children were removed from alms houses to congregate institutions, maintained by private charity with public support. The indigency of parents was equated with neglect. Juvenile Courts did not escape a web of prejudice based on the poverty of parents. Despite faith in individualized justice for children, the admission of family records and hearsay testimony, reinforced distrust of indigent parents in the Juvenile Courts.

Poverty and dependence encouraged the filing of neglect petitions by schools, neighbors, and social agencies. They, also, affected the recommendations by probation officers in the court for preventive work with families, referrals for court action, and recommendations for the removal of children. Finally, these same factors affected the likelihood of acceptance by voluntary agencies that chose to work with "stable" families. Parents and children in greatest need were often excluded as poor prospects for help.

Even when the New Deal provided regular aid to more children in their own homes through social security legislation, the Juvenile Court continued as the last refuge for many thousands of children. Although aid to neglected children had been one of the two primary goals of the Juvenile Court movement, legislatures, public agencies, and private charities had been slow to provide help. More interest was always shown in correcting or punishing delinquents who were seen as a threat to the community.

Some striking similarities appear between the rise and fall of the movement for juvenile justice with the growth and decline of Federal action on behalf of child care. A few years after the first White House Conference (1909), Congress established the Children's Bureau. Under the strong leadership of Grace Abbott, the Bureau was seen as the primary agency to collect facts, to set standards for child care, and to serve as an advocate for poor children. This pioneering effort produced valuable and lasting benefits. Yet, paradoxically, with the enactment of New Deal legislation that provided for poor children in their own homes, the role of the Children's Bureau declined. The Bureau, with its loss of effectiveness, was defeated in its battle for the administration of Aid to Dependent Children (ADC). The Bureau of Public Assistance, under the Social Security Board, became a public information lobby, while the Children's Bureau was decimated without a decent burial. During the Nixon administration, many of its functions were transferred to other agencies, and it has all but disappeared under the Reagan administration, although the original Congressional legislation creating the Bureau remains on the books.

The Slow Rise of Foster Home Care

Substitute homes for neglected children were developed more slowly in the East than in other parts of the country where voluntary sectarian institutions were fewer and less powerful.

Although 1,000 dependent children had been placed in foster homes by the New York City Welfare Department before World War I, the program was shut down under political pressure, when attacked by sectarian groups as an invasion of their domain. It was not until after World War II that the use of foster homes was widely embraced. They were welcomed only as old institutions became obsolete and when new ones were no longer built by charitable agencies. They became a necessity as cases of neglected children increased in staggering numbers.[4] Finally, the high proportion of black children and opposition to racial discrimination confronted the child-care system. The use of black and white foster homes provided an acceptable answer to both black and white communities for different reasons.

New questions about the use of foster care began to appear in the 1960s. "The limbo of foster home care" became a subject for concern. A study of 100 children in foster care described parental neglect after placement as dominating their lives. Parents had deserted periodically or permanently and most of the children had been in foster care for more than 8 years.

In 1979, the Federal government reported that of the half-million children in foster care, more than a quarter-million had been separated from their natural families for more than 2 years; 100,000 children had been separated for more than 6 years. Fifty thousand children in foster care who had been freed for adoption had not been placed in adoptive homes. To be lost in the limbo of foster care was not limited to children in foster homes,

but foster home care became the object of special criticism as an insufficient substitute for permanent homes. It was reported that as children
remained in foster care they became less and less adoptable, and that after
foster care placement had been ordered, little was done to strengthen natural
families for possible reunion.[5]

Many legitimate questions about children in foster home care became
louder and demanded scapegoats. By 1980, the benign image of the foster
home parent was transformed from an admirable substitute parent to an object for suspicion. A spillover, without adequate data, described the foster
home child as more likely to become delinquent or mentally ill. Prevention
of placement with too little differentiation of the needs of children was
placed high on the agenda of state and local governments. Preventive services were used as tardy bandaids but there were few efforts to confront the
underlying causes for neglect within the family.

The Many Definitions of Neglect

State legislatures easily enacted broad definitions of *child neglect*. They
included physical injury before the term, *child abuse* was added. Some
states included emotional deprivation. All listed the failure to clothe, feed,
or provide necessary medical care. They were generally interpreted to cover
leaving a young child alone while a parent visited friends or a neighborhood
bar. Sexual misconduct in or outside the home was treated as neglect even
when not specifically defined. Incest within the family was not mentioned.
It was a taken-for-granted taboo. None of the statutory definitions, no matter how fully or artfully drawn, prepared judges for what they would hear
and see. Neglect cases covered every mistake, error, and crime perpetrated
by adults—from the trivial to mutilation and murder.

Physical Abuse and Neglect

Judges were gripped and horrified by evidence of physical injuries inflicted by parents on their children or on one another. At first, a stern judicial lecture followed by the temporary removal of a physically injured child
seemed just punishment of the parent and adequate protection for the child.
Later, long-term removal of a child was widely approved. It took time to
realize the hurts inflicted by such decisions on children and parents. The

bedraggled terror of a parent mowed down by many cares and the awful fears of the child began to appear more clearly. Swift, punitive action held features of too-easy virtue for the judge.

Tony was only 10 when he was brought before the court for placement as a neglected child. His father had deserted the family and the home was overcrowded and dirty. Charged with neglect, the mother screamed that she did not want to be bothered with Tony anymore, and that the court should take him. Although Tony had suffered physical abuse at her hands and heard her words, he clutched at her, begging to go home. The mother did not relent and Tony was placed. He waited month after month for visits that never came. Becoming sadder and more of a loner, he told his worker, "There's no use in trying to be good." His mother's abandonment was all that mattered to Tony.

A 15-year-old lived with his alcoholic grandmother, without adequate food or clothing, in a filthy apartment. Still, he begged not to be removed, saying he was needed to protect his grandmother and to help his drug-addicted mother when she was released from prison. Realizing that the court would not leave him in this home, he blurted out, "I know my home is considered bad, but it has good things, too. No one here understands, because you haven't lived there." He stuck to his guns and proved right, eventually finishing school, securing work, and returning home to care for his family.

Child Abuse

The Juvenile Court dealt with many forms of neglect. But, the term *child abuse* was not used until the 1950s. In 1950, the first alarm was sounded by a Philadelphia hospital in a report on serious, repeated injuries to infants returned to their parents, following unexplained earlier injuries. A few years later, the words took on broader dimensions from the pioneering study by Dr. Henry Kempe and Dr. Brandt Steele on 300 children who "failed to thrive." Many were found to have suffered parental rejection. This remarkable team of a pediatrician and a psychiatrist saw the parents as lonely people who would not be "dangerous," if they were given supportive help from a trusted adult. These physicians found that with such help, only a small proportion (later estimated at 10%) remained "dangerous," so that their children should be removed.

In 1961, the Academy of Pediatricians recognized dangers from child abuse, and the Children's Bureau campaigned to require physicians to report "suspicion of abuse." Four years later, the AMA pronounced that physical abuse was a more likely cause of death in children than well-known diseases. Abuse cases filtered into the Juvenile Court slowly. When they came, incredulity, horror, and anger brought a death-like silence into the courtroom. At first, judges found willful injury of a child by a parent hard to believe. One colleague told me of a mother charged with breaking the arm of her infant daughter. The mother claimed she had dropped the baby accidentally, and now wanted her back. The judge said he could not believe any woman who had carried an infant for 9 months before birth would willfully injure her baby after birth, and he returned the baby. Ten days later, the baby was pronounced dead on arrival at a second hospital from a head injury, and the mother was charged with homicide.

The first child abuse case brought before me was in 1965.[6] A grandmother had noticed bruises and sores on the legs of her 3-year-old grandchild Marion when she dropped in to visit. She called the police and, when the child was hospitalized, the doctors noted "suspicion of abuse." Court investigation disclosed that the child had been hospitalized three times during the 3 months since the child's mother had taken her from the grandmother to live with her and her new husband. The stepfather had taken Marion to the emergency room of the first hospital telling the physician that she had slipped in the bath. Alhough suspicious of abuse, the physician released her to the stepfather after emergency treatment. The mother had taken her to a second hospital for treatment, but remained silent when asked what had caused the bruises and lesions on the child's legs. "Suspicion of abuse" was noted in the record, but Marion was released to the mother. When the physician at the second hospital was questioned in court as to why he had not pressed for an explanation, he replied, "I'm not expected to investigate." In the third hospital, Marion was described as "sweet, docile, and petrified."

Physicians and hospitals were not alone in seeking to avoid involvement in child abuse cases. As states and localities established "Protective Services," workers with large caseloads and little legal guidance feared court action. They preferred plea bargaining with a parent suspected of child abuse. They would tell the parent, "If you agree to voluntary placement of your child, no complaint will be filed in court." After such a "voluntary" placement, the parent could subsequently reclaim the child without facing a trial on the abuse charge. Judges were also hesitant to remove children from their homes even after trials had proved abuse. They preferred to issue stern warnings against further abuse. The hope and the prayer that the warning would prevent further abuse left the child without protective supervision.

Changing theories about the causation of child abuse were of little practical help to judges who had to decide whether a specific child could be safely returned home. Theories of causation included an unwanted and difficult pregnancy, a child who looked different from other family members, uncontrolled discipline by one parent, a time of unusual stress for a family, atypical and provocative behavior on the part of a child and the mental disability of a parent. Very young children, according to Professor David Gil, who did a national study on child abuse, tended to be more seriously injured, and fatal injuries were nearly exclusively limited to the very young.

Professor Gil also provided a broader perspective. He believed that community failure to meet the needs of poor children and their families constituted massive neglect far greater than that resulting from injuries by individual parents. He contended that social problems resulting from inadequate education, insufficient medical care, and substandard living conditions increased the propensity of parents to discharge angry feelings against their children.[7,8]

Besides the conflicting theories about causation, the Juvenile Court judge had to face questions not answered during a trial. Did the parent really want this child returned home, or would he or she be more relieved if the child was placed? Would the parent accept services? Was this child at risk if returned home? Did the judge have the right to go beyond the complaint, and consider the risk to siblings still at home? Uncertainty of prediction cast many doubts on the rightness of decisions involving child abuse.

The number of child abuse cases brought to court increased steadily.[9] After lengthy debate, Congress enacted the first national "Child Abuse, Prevention and Treatment Act" in 1974. It defined child abuse and neglect as the physical or mental injury, neglectful treatment, or maltreatment of a child under 18 by a person responsible for the child's welfare.[10] In 1977, Dr. Bertram Brown of the National Institute for Mental Health commented that while compulsory education dated back 150 years, and opposition to child labor arose 75 years ago, America was only beginning to set limits on physical and emotional abuse of children by parents. He estimated that 6 out of every 1,000 children being born would suffer such abuse.[11]

Abuse That Kills

Of the many thousands of children who appeared before me, the face of one small child has remained unforgettable and chastening. Roxanne had been placed at birth, after her homeless mother had threatened suicide. Three years later, her mother asked for Roxanne's return, saying her new husband would support her, their baby, and Roxanne. When the case appeared on my calendar in December 1968, the probation officer stated there was no need for a hearing. She explained that the placement had expired and that the foster care agency was not requesting an extension because it approved discharge to the mother. When the mother, her husband, Roxanne, and the agency workers appeared, the caseworker testified she knew the mother and child, and recommended that Roxanne be returned home. Her supervisor stated she had nothing to add. The stepfather testified he was able and ready to support. The law guardian asked no questions. Seeing Roxanne resting happily in her mother's lap, this seemed like a fairytale beginning for a long court day.

Three months later, Roxanne's body was found in the East River and the stepfather was charged with her torture and death. A month after I had discharged the child to her mother, the former foster parents had reported signs of abuse to the foster care agency. The supervising agency noted "suspicion of abuse," but was dilatory in taking action. A judge, new to the case, paroled Roxanne to the mother pending investigation. A warrant was issued by a third judge when the mother failed to appear. The media blamed the judge who had paroled Roxanne to the mother. Almost everyone, including the senior physician at the agency, ran for cover. Only a few judges agreed to join in an open letter setting forth the facts. Some disapproved of responding to attacks on the judiciary. One phoned me at home to express admiration for the proposed letter but added that, of course, she could not be expected to sign it because her reappointment would soon be under consideration. A committee appointed by the Appellate Division, after lengthy hearings, presented a waffling report. With general recommendations for stronger court administration, an end to the rotation of judges, and an increase in warrant officers, the report placed major responsibility on the judge who had paroled Roxanne and touched lightly on the shortcomings of the custodial agency.

It was only after Roxanne's death that information was assembled that might have prevented it. Neighbors reported frequent beatings. The foster parents told of injuries reported to the agency. Old records, collected at this late date, showed that the mother had been hospitalized 7 years before Roxanne was born for outbursts against teachers and fellow pupils. She had also been in a state hospital after several suicidal attempts.

The story of Roxanne continued to flash back when I heard arguments against intervention in "the family" as though all families were identical. One day in 1977, Dr. Kempe told of being charged by a lawyer with violating the rights of a mother by observing and acting on signs that predicted an infant might be at risk of abuse, without first securing the mother's consent to observe. Dr. Kempe answered that when a patient came to a physician because of a sore throat, the physician did not ask for consent to examine eyes, do a blood test, or other tests he felt necessary for diagnosis and treatment. He believed that to deny the same right to protect an infant, born or unborn, was inconsistent with his duties as a physician.

Twenty years after beginning his work on children at risk, Dr. Kempe still felt forced to ask, "Does every community need a martyred child before it will provide preventive services?" Then he added that not to be reinjured or killed was not a sufficient goal!

Sexual Abuse

Avoidance of confronting parental abuse intensified when abuse within a family alleged incest. Mothers, who had tried desperately not to see that a husband entered a daughter's bed, became fearful and refused to testify against their husbands. Children were silent, terrified that disclosures would lead to imprisonment of their fathers. In the 1970s, anti-interventionists claimed that lasting harm from incest had not been proven. But the comforting myth of the dirty old man near the schoolyard was slowly replaced by studies showing that sexual abuse was a serious problem within many family walls. One such study reported that of 200 prostitutes, 59% had been involved in incestuous relations. A majority of these girls came from white, middle-class backgrounds. [12]

In a few court cases, the tragic impact of incest on small children was dramatic. In one family two girls, aged 5 and 8, who were subjected to their father's attacks when he was drunk, were first diagnosed as mentally retarded, but showed amazing improvement when hospitalized. There was even hope that the 5-year-old would develop normally if protected from further sexual abuse. The 8-year-old, burdened by dreams of monsters and of being dead, also became cheerful in the hospital.

Recently, a study of all psychiatric patients, discharged over an 18-month period from a university teaching hospital, reported that 43% had suffered physical or sexual abuse. Of the abused patients, 90% had been abused by family members.[13] One cynical or knowledgeable commentator, noting the succession of fleeting national interest in the problems of children and youth, predicted that in 1980 "sexual abuse had emerged as the topic of concern for the coming year, particularly in light of recent funding by the Federal government in this area."[14]

Emotional Abuse

Affection for his parents had only died in him because it had been killed anew, again and again, each time that it tried to spring.[15]

Just as professionals and courts began to acknowledge the existence of parental physical abuse, they drew back from involvement in emotional abuse. It was called "too vague a concept" for judicial intervention. A few advocates of parental rights argued for the return home of children as therapy for the parents. The concept of the special meaning of time for children removed from home was not applied to children left in homes where they were subjected to continuing emotional neglect.

Adolescents, who had suffered emotional abuse, often accused themselves rather than their parents. Barbara, a 13-year-old runaway, cried out in court, "It's all my fault. My mother and father quarreled many times. Then one night, I heard him say, 'It's all your fault, I didn't want her. Now I'm leaving. You're stuck with her.' So that's what I am." Another adolescent, neglected by her mother, had found comfort in memories of her grandmother. "My grandmother was a woman. She understood what it was like to be lonely and frightened. That's why she took me in. My mother is a woman in body, but she is not a woman in mind. It's not her fault. She did not bring me up, but it's not my fault either. I can't accept her ways. If I did, my life would be just like hers, a piece of paper floating in the street."

The ongoing harms to a child from emotional neglect or abuse were the most difficult to assess. Unlike physical abuse, it was intangible, elusive. The emotional emptiness of a parent could create such distances that a child became an orphan within the home. A 17-year-old angered by the crying of her 3-month-old, thrust a nipple into his mouth and shook him, screaming, "Look at you, having a temper tantrum." Reminded that he was just a baby, the mother replied, "He's older than you think!" and walked away. Emotional abuse took many forms. Mothers who had provided affectionate care to infants, rejected them when they showed signs of independence or when new babies were born.

Few parents acknowledged emotional abuse of their children or saw how deeply they hurt their children. In a unique letter, one mother who had reluctantly accepted her son home after years of placement, wrote:

> ...there just isn't room for both Cecil and I here. Either someone has to find him a place to stay or I am not coming home anymore. It is truly not Cecil's fault...I am not a good mother because I just don't have the proper feelings or something...If my place was larger and there was room where Cecil would be out of the way sometime, perhaps I would feel different, but I can't be sure of that even. He is a good boy and tries very hard and he really does deserve a better life, but I can't give it to him. His life has been pretty bad but mine hasn't been any picnic either. I can't really care much what happens next. My conscience is very obliging; it bothers me only when I want it to ... I don't have any future anyway and what little is left of my life I want to be as happy as I can make it ... I really want to see Cecil settled in a nice home where he can be reasonably happy and where he will have a chance to make something of his life but not at the expense of my own.

Such self-scrutiny was far different from the ordinary reasons given by parents when seeking placement of a child. Acts of misbehavior were magnified to the bewilderment of a child. When the death of a grandmother forced a mother to take back her 12-year-old son, she called him "bad things," including "son of a prostitute." Terrified that she was not his mother, he ran away. At the clinic, he spoke of his grandmother as the only person who had ever loved him. She appeared to him at night, but when he reached out, she was not there. One night, after his mother called on the devil to come and get him, the devil appeared in his room. When questioned, the mother's response was that she had never wanted Jose, that her pregnancy had been painful, and that he should be put away until he became a man and could take care of himself.

More even than in cases of physical abuse, involvement by a court in emotional abuse cases ran counter to the general belief in the universal love of parents for their children. Still, in welfare departments and in courts, mothers appeared, one by one, who did not like a child, who turned away from a particular child, who could not express love or protect a child from harm. And, their children also appeared, one by one, stunted, hurt, and fearful.

There was little guidance for a judge to know when emotional starvation would freeze a child's capacity to feel, when a hardening process would set in irrevocably. Advocates of "liberty interests" for parents offered only the promise that a child's wounds would heal themselves. The erosion of a child's ability to function, the desperate awareness of not being wanted, and the loss of self-worth were, too often, overlooked.

Estimating harm to a child from emotional abuse was seen by many public defenders as requiring "complex calculations impossible for judges to make." This condescension toward judges was supported by the self-confidence of theorists who never witnessed what happened to adolescents whose vitality had been sapped by daily emotional abuse. In contrast, the court clinic wrote of one boy, "Though some people might call him a psychopath, his reactions may be seen as natural and logical. He needs primarily a place where he will be accepted with open arms."

Some professionals began to study the consequences of emotional neglect. *Psychologically unavailable mothering* was the term used to describe mothers among all classes, although it was most frequently reported among young, poor, unmarried mothers. Psychological effects on children included aggression, anger, and hyperactivity. But there was a lack of will or services to intervene, except when deprivations or abuse were life-threatening.

How little was known about the effects of emotional abuse on adolescents was summed up by one psychiatrist in 1977: "We know only in general terms about the increased delinquency rate, the increased pregnancy rate, the increased use of drugs, and the increased suicide rate among adolescents."[16]

Children—Uncounted and Unseen

There were many confrontations between public and private agencies in the eastern United States about the development of public services. Insistence on control of care for neglected children by voluntary agencies was buttressed by their belief that they had rendered and would always render higher quality services than the public could command. Public bodies acted with timidity when confronted by voluntary agencies, especially when such agencies were under powerful sectarian auspices.

The right to control care included the right to accept or reject individual children referred by the Juvenile Court. The absence of information about children denied appropriate care made advocacy for them all but impossible. Judges saw tragic individual cases of neglected children, wrongly placed or held for long periods in congregate care without family contacts. But these children were uncounted and many were returned to damaging home situations.

Statistics on the disposition of neglected children have been largely nonexistent. As early as 1937, two distinguished researchers in child welfare wrote, " no community has squarely faced the problem of caring for unimproved cases that have been closed or rejected by voluntary agencies, and, therefore, we have no means of knowing the size of the group of neglected cases."[17] This is still all too true.

Juvenile Court judges generally accepted whatever services were provided and attempted little independent scrutiny. Although the New York law directed that judges visit institutions to which they sent children, such visits had generally taken place on ceremonial occasions. In 1936, a group of New York judges, concerned by how little they knew, requested and secured the appointment of a Committee of Judges on Institutions. This action was not welcomed by the child-care agencies.[18] Anxiety was expressed by three sectarian federations about the investigation of voluntary agencies and one sectarian federation denied admission to committee staff.[19]

The Presiding Justice felt it necessary to agree that the committee of judges would not examine the composition of boards or the finances of the voluntary agencies. It was also agreed that the committee would not evaluate the work of the agencies. To conceal its lack of records on children, one agency outside the city had them brought up to date by a compliant probation officer who used old and out-dated court records to make the agency records look satisfactory.

Unannounced visits by the judges were met with polite deference. These were eye-opening visits. The gloom of some institutions for neglected children was intensified by endless memorial plaques to benefactors, more appropriate to chapels for the dead than to a home for living children. The same gloom arose from the heavy table dishes, set on dark oilcloth and in the near-empty recreations rooms. In one institution three sets of dishes showed the high value placed on benefactors rather than on staff and children. The good dishes were for the volunteer ladies who visited occasionally. A second, simpler set was for staff, whereas an assortment of chipped remainders supplemented by unbreakable metal dishes were used for the children. The ghostly air of the place became heavy as the director pointed to children and spoke of their problems as though the children were not alive and were not listening.

Brutality toward neglected children was seen only on a few visits. But on one cold, winter day a colleague and I saw neglected boys at an institution draped in soiled sheets, standing in line on the playground as punishment for having wet their beds. The director was confident that this punishment would correct their "misbehavior." In contrast to that experience, we also saw how the headmistress of another sectarian institution had added color and beauty to every corner of an old fortress-like institution. Her humor and love for the girls seemed to touch everyone in the place with magic.

The staff study of child-care institutions for the Committee of Justices, a first for the court, was completed in 1941. It pointed up the vast differences experienced by children, committed by judges who did not know what their decisions would mean. The differences were not only in the range of kindness and concern. They reflected policy decisions on how long a neglected child should be kept in custody. Five agencies kept children from 2 to 4 years; one held children for over 4 years; 7 agencies held them for less than 3 years. Some agencies had foster homes and adoption services, whereas others relied only on congregate care. Vocational training varied from real programs to what was only unpaid maintenance work.

Among the most disturbing findings was the pervasive racial discrimination practiced by agencies for neglected children. When the Board of Justice was informed, it voted that voluntary agencies should meet the needs of all neglected children. But little good resulted at that time. The voluntary agencies responded with continuing opposition to interference in what they regarded as their domain. This stance had long been tolerated, if not supported, by the state welfare department that had neither reported nor taken issue with racial discrimination practiced against neglected children. Although cognizant of the critical lack of services for black children, the State Board reports showed no effort to open the doors of voluntary agencies. It avoided the problem.

State reports did not dig below the surface in other areas. They chose to concentrate on financial requirements and record keeping more than on the life experiences of children in institutions. Recommendations for improvements were also tempered in accordance with the political power of the groups who sponsored the voluntary agencies; least was demanded from the more powerful and most from those with least clout.

Although the State Board respectfully recommended more than a single caseworker for 261 girls in one agency, it criticized a caseload of more than 35 girls in a smaller agency under different auspices. It approved one registered nurse to supervise 239 infants in a famous foundling home, and complimented it on discontinuing the practice of holding indigent, unmarried girls to work out their maternity costs after their babies were born. The State Board took contradictory positions in regard to religious practices. Noting that one nonsectarian agency had 18% of non-Protestant girls, it urged provision for religious training in their faith. No such recommendation was made to a Catholic institution that accepted Protestant and Jewish girls. Although the Board praised one agency for adding social workers and educators to its board, it said nothing to powerful boards without professional members.

Abject surrender of child-care principles appeared in one state report on a sectarian institution that mingled young, neglected Puerto Rican girls with older, white delinquents. Without criticism, this report only repeated the agency's explanation that those "neglected children were victims of unfortunate sex experiences or had come from an environment...[of] gross 'immorality'."

The Awesome Power of Rejection

Apart from the inadequacy, disparity and discrimination in programs for neglected children, black holes in the system were caused by repeated rejections of children referred for placement. Some children were accepted promptly, whereas others waited endlessly in "temporary" shelters or were returned to destructive homes. Judges could plead but not command acceptance of a child. Workers in the shelters saw the hurts when children felt that there was something wrong with them because no one wanted them. One worker wrote of the increasing silence of a boy after each rejection; "He had a nervous mouth movement, tensing his lips and gritting his teeth.

A general lethargy pins him down with an expression that seems to say, 'It is not worth the effort to even work for something.'"

Workers in agencies confident in their judgments about which children to accept, often did not see the children rejected and only looked at "the records." When one agency agreed to see Ada "to please the judge," the visit caused only further sadness for the girl. The worker began the interview with a reprimand to this 15-year-old for not having written more regularly to her parents. Reminded by the probation officer that the record showed that Ada's father had deserted and that her mother was in a state hospital, the worker took a different tack. She announced that the agency did not accept children who had no families so that Ada should not feel personally rejected. Dismissed, Ada whispered to the court worker, "They are not very nice people."

Agencies were chary in disclosing their reasons for rejections to the Juvenile Court. A stock phrase stated, "The child is not suited to our programs." But the social agencies were not single villains in the neglect of neglected children. Legislative bodies, judges, and administrative officials each played a role.

On a train to Albany in the 1950s, I commented to the Commissioner of Welfare on the fortunate reduction in neglect complaints in view of the shortages of facilities. Obviously amazed by my naiveté, he replied, "I can create an epidemic of those cases any day. All I have to do is to issue a directive lifting the ban to my staff against reporting neglect."

Neither the state legislature nor the state executive departments would support the establishment of essential public services for neglected children. Juvenile Court judges, too, were ineffective representatives on behalf of neglected children. A few opposed intervention on principle. One opposed even preventive services at intake in the court, saying: "If the neglect is not flagrant, whose business is it to interfere in the family?" More found that neglect cases were protracted and thankless and preferred delinquency cases.[20] A well-intentioned reform provided that neglected children could be excused from being present at hearings. This made it easier for judges not to see the hurts inflicted on neglected children. Judges also found themselves subject to erratic responses from the public. Demands for immediate harsh punishment of neglectful parents quickly changed to widespread disinterest in the absence of a dramatic media story.

Distancing Neglected Children

The Juvenile Court had enjoyed immunity from criticism in its treatment of neglected children during the first half of the 20th century. In the East this was in accord with obeisance to private charity that controlled their care. But this immunity faded as the court system accepted growing distancing between neglected children and those expected to render services. Early signs of change appeared in the polite ousting of "lady bountifuls" who had combined genuine solicitude for individual children with officious interference. Next, the laying on of hands was widely discredited as too paternalistic. The employment of paid staff, with or without professional training, replaced the friendly visitors, and staff became the arbiters for recommendations to the court. Charitable boards, also, distanced themselves from programs under their auspices. Brief downtown luncheon meetings to review budgets and investments with businessmen largely replaced involvement in the programs for the care of children.

With agency workers no longer seeing themselves as supervisors of substitute parents, youth in foster care often felt no one considered their problems. When they "aged out," no longer entitled to public funding and were discharged to live on their own, they felt doubly alone. Follow-ups on what happened to them were few, and these youths were again lost from sight.[21]

Each of these steps prepared the way to transfer decision making to distant public administrators, and to reduce the discretionary powers of the court in the dispositions of neglected children. A similar process followed with regard to the placement of delinquent children.

The reorganization and redistribution of authority for the disposition of neglected children failed to assure better care. In 1970, as 30 years earlier, a New York study showed that inappropriate placements still hovered at over 50%. The Federal Department of Health, Education and Welfare acknowledged in 1979 that little was known about the extent of either institutional abuse or family neglect.

Chapter 5
The Search for Permanence

Parental Rights

Parental rights were so absolute in American tradition and law that child welfare played a timid role in the protection of children from neglect and abuse within their homes. Throughout recorded history the unquestioned power of parents imposed many forms of destructive permanence on their children. Other countries had allowed exposure of unwanted infants (usually female), the sale of children into slavery, and the mutilation of children to enhance their success as beggars. For poor children in this country, the workhouse and the poorhouse provided "permanence" until replaced by indenture, orphanages, and eventually foster care or adoption.

Permanence was not regarded as a responsibility of charitable or public institutions that held children of the poor. Even with the establishment of the Juvenile Court and far into the 20th century, the only permanence for neglected or abused children was the permanence of poverty. When removed from their homes, children remained in designated slots year after year. Little note was paid to whether parents visited or showed any interest in them or their future.

Successive methods of substitute care were presented as the best alternative to "bad" parents, each in turn promising least cost to the taxpayer. Although little interest was shown in parents after removal of a child, the legal rights of birth parents were zealously guarded. Except when surrender or long-time abandonment freed a small number of infants for adoption, removal of a child from birth parents was treated as a temporary measure.

Day after day in court, the loneliness and terror of children removed from neglectful or abusive parents mocked the good intentions of rescue operations. Judges could remove a child from immediate harm but orders for foster care often outlasted childhood. Children disappeared from the sight of judges and were not seen again unless they were brought back for running away or for some other misbehavior while in placement. Then, if they would, judges could gain a sense of the bleak, uprooted lives that had told these children that there was no one who cared what happened to them.

About 20 years ago, 10-year-old Ronnie stood alone, in torn sneakers, charged with delinquency. He had been caught in a clumsy attempt to steal a pair of shoes. His father's whereabouts were unknown; his mother was serving a long prison sentence. After the mother's arrest Ronnie had been left with a mentally ill aunt until she was hospitalized. Then he had been turned over by Welfare to an indigent uncle who agreed to share his furnished room. Welfare provided nothing for Ronnie's clothing. In detention, Ronnie was seen as a normal boy eager for friends. The clinic described his need for warmth and personal care. But, this was 1960, and only temporary shelter and institutionalization were possible. Ronnie had no one to whom he could turn; he did not cry or protest as he was taken out of court for his first official placement.

Temporary Care

Shelters and detention provided first-aid stations for the court. But, they were frightening depositories for children removed from everyone they knew. Even when children were old enough to understand words, they were not told what they might expect. Because they were meant to be "temporary" placements, brothers and sisters were taken in buses or taxis by probation officers or court clerks at the end of each day, and dropped off wherever vacancies had been found. This often meant separation from one another on the same day that the children were removed from home. They did not know how long they would stay or what would happen to them next. They were not seen again in court until some long-term plan was worked out, if then.

Shelter care was, and remains, big business in child care. Yet, even when it lasted for many months, "temporary" care was little more than custodial in the sectarian shelters and those run by the S.P.C.C. A study in 1948 reported that two-thirds of the children had remained beyond the approved 90-day limit.[1] Some children had been left in shelter for more than 6 months. Most of the buildings used for temporary care were described at that time as "dreary, drab...and in a few places grim and Dickens-like." Children slept in rows of beds. The bathrooms were frequently dirty and malodorous. Rigid rules and locked doors created a jail-like atmosphere. Little or no privacy was allowed. Impersonal controls and lack of trained staff made attention to the needs and fears of children impossible.

The 1948 study presented straightforward findings, but, in accordance with traditions and "good manners" prevalent in child welfare, it did not identify the shelters. They were only listed as "A," "B," "C," and so forth. Charitable agencies were treated with kid gloves. They were "entitled" to anonymity. As late as 1982, when the Citizens' Committee for Children of New York used computerized public data to rank the performance of voluntary agencies, it was rebuked by public and voluntary officials for identifying agencies.

Endless holding of children in temporary shelters continued, with few questions asked. In 1974, a Task Force I chaired reported that, between August 1973 and August 1974, in New York City, 8,934 children had been in temporary care, and the number was growing. They included children placed for emergency care, awaiting findings by the Juvenile Court, and awaiting long-term placement after judgments had been made. The Department of Welfare still referred all children to voluntary agencies for long-term care, before it would consider public services under its own auspices. These referrals, made one at a time, dragged on while children waited.

Although increasingly supported by public funds, the voluntary shelters continued to be selective as to which children they would accept. They sent daily listings to the Department that listed as acceptable: "White, either sex, newborn"; "Negro, Protestant, female 0–8 years"; "White, Puerto Rican, female 0–3 years"; "White, Jewish, 0–2 years." Added conditions excluded physically or mentally handicapped children. The one public shelter had become the dumping ground for a majority of the "problem children" and a high proportion of minority children.[2] In brief, temporary shelters for children, like jails, continued to be relics of past decades where community neglect inflicted pain, pervasive but unseen.[3]

Long-Term Care Without Exit

Although social agencies proclaimed devotion to the family, they continued to separate brothers and sisters according to rigid admission policies and the location of empty beds. When brothers and sisters were initially placed separately there was no assurance they would be reunited, or that they would be allowed to visit one another. Three abandoned children of drug addicts were placed separately for emergency shelter. On my review 18 months later in 1967, the 8-year-old boy was in a foster home that hoped to adopt him. His 7-year-old brother was in another foster home not interested in providing permanent care. The youngest, a 2-year-old girl, was still in a congregate shelter. They had not seen one another during this period. Although all were under the care of the same voluntary agency, no one had done anything to unite them. The agency worker spoke only of how hard it would be to find a permanent home for the middle child, because he showed evidence of a "Negro mixture." Although this child, light in color, had been placed with a white family, the excuse for no visits between the brothers was the difference in pigmentation. The 2-year-old girl had not been considered for placement with either of her brothers, nor was she referred for adoption.

Although the court demanded better plans for these three children, I discovered there was also a 13-year-old sister, Mary, who had been in foster care for 9 years under the care of the same agency. She had never been visited by any relative. When pressed for some permanent plan for her, the agency announced that this child had been damaged in her present foster home, and that institutional care was indicated. Although the agency had done nothing to correct the "damaging" foster home situation until the court inquiry, the worker aggressively added, "We must forcefully state our protest to removing Mary from our agency."

This story was not unusual. Neglected and abused sisters and brothers were ripped apart and left apart. Racial discrimination against siblings of different pigmentation within a family was occasionally used to justify permanent separations. The assertion of a vested property right to continuing custody reflected more than the personal arrogance of the worker. It reflected the sense of agency power and a property interest that resisted any court action on behalf of Mary.

The Child's Right to a Permanent Home

Recognition of injuries done to neglected children removed from parents dawned slowly in child welfare, in government bureaucracies, and in the courts. Two major factors bound children to impermanence. First, a lack of information about children and the absence of court responsibility for their well-being, after initial removal to agency care; and second, obeisance to the rights of birth parents. Children were left indefinitely in foster care, even when there were no homes to which they could be returned. Despite few or no contacts between parents and a child after placement, courts were reluctant to find "abandonment" unless they also found "a settled purpose to forego forever all parental rights."

In 1959, two landmark steps were taken on behalf of children in foster care. That year, two scholars reported the diminishing likelihood of a child's return to natural parents with each passing year in placement.[4] It was also in 1959 that the Citizens' Committee for Children of New York took the giant leap of sponsoring legislation, drafted by its counsel to create a new category on behalf of the "permanently neglected child." After extensive negotiations with voluntary agencies, public agencies, and the courts, the first "permanent child neglect" statutes were enacted.[5]

The "permanently neglected child" was narrowly defined in the statute to meet objections of voluntary agencies. The parents must have failed substantially and continuously to maintain contact with the child for more than a year, *and* failed to plan for the child's future, although physically and financially able to do so, notwithstanding diligent efforts by the agency to strengthen the child-parent relationship. The original statute allowed only authorized agencies to bring actions on behalf of a "permanently neglected child." It provided due process protections to parents. Its goal was to find a way to allow adoption without the consent of parents for children "left emotionally adrift (when) their inevitable lot was custodial care."[6]

The necessity for the permanent neglect law became more apparent when the Family Court Act was enacted in 1962; it required judicial review of all neglected children in placement for more than 18 months. Judges could then see what happened to a child, to siblings, and to the family during placement. They could question why so many children, unvisited or abandoned, had not been freed for adoption. Later, the Family Court Act was amended (1971) to require that the reviewing judge, in each case, determine whether a child should be returned home, freed for adoption, or continued in foster care.

Further amendments strengthening the permanent neglect statute were enacted, one by one, over a period of years between 1971 and 1976. In 1971, the Family Court was permitted to waive the requirement that the custodial agency must make diligent efforts to strengthen the parent-child relationship on proof that such efforts would be injurious to a child.[7] Two years later, the conditions for termination were broadened to allow proof of failure by parents to maintain meaningful contacts with a child for more than a year or to plan for the child's future, although physically and financially able to do so. [8] With the change of the word from "and" to "or" more children were freed.

Two major amendments were enacted in 1976. One allowed termination if the parent was mentally ill and impartial medical evidence established that the illness would continue for the forseeable future.[9] The second allowed foster parents, who wished to adopt a child who was in their care for over 18 months to initiate proceedings to terminate parental rights.[10,11,12] Until this time, foster home parents had been held at arms length by statutes, courts, and social agencies. They were denied the right to initiate adoption proceedings for children in their care.[13,14]

At hearings to terminate parental rights, judges could no longer rely on the comforting assumption that their decisions for placement involved only the temporary removal of a child. Easy decisions were possible only when parents had disappeared or agreed to termination. Repeatedly, notice of a termination proceeding triggered parental feelings of guilt and loss. Even parents who had failed to visit children in foster care held on to them as possessions or as their last proof of parenthood. Some parents, who protested termination, seemed to accept defeat with relief when the court, rather than they themselves, made the decision.

Some natural or "birth" parents battled for their rights to children they had rarely visited, and the cases dragged through the courts for years, so that the children often outgrew the possibility of a permanent home through adoption. Case after case portrayed tragedies in the past lives of natural parents. They also revealed how little hope there would be for children tied to parents unable to function as parents.

David had been placed in a foster home when his mother was committed as seriously retarded, according to the state hospital where he was born. The mother had rarely visited him and was living in a furnished room with a baby by a different father. When the foster parents who had cared for David since infancy sought to adopt him at the age of 9, the mother protested that David belonged to her. The court clinic found the mother profoundly retarded, depressed, and incapable of caring for her son. David, a child of superior intelligence with musical gifts, spoke of his foster parents as "mother and daddy." He pleaded to remain with them and not be forced to see "my other mother."

To wound a deeply troubled parent once more in order to provide a permanent home for a child was an awesome, new judicial task. In one termination case, counsel for the parents urged special consideration for the parents, because they were "poor and black." The parents were, indeed, both poor and black. They were also long-time heroin addicts who lived like nomads in the city. They had rarely visited or contacted their three children, each placed successively as neglected over a period of more than 5 years. Counsel for the parents argued that the failure to contact the children should be evaluated in the light of the "class mores of poor, black, unskilled persons," and that they should not be required to conform "with the customs of bourgeois urban existence." My holding that poor, black children were entitled to equal protection under the law did not lessen the pain of termination for these parents. Their mute acceptance of defeat was far more poignant than the argument of counsel.

It was small wonder that uncertainty and pretensions to wisdom were reflected in judicial decisions. One Solomonic judge ordered that a child's life be cut in half. He dismissed the petition to terminate parental rights against the mother who had been hospitalized repeatedly over 7 years for psychotic episodes. In the same decision he gave custody to the foster parents, but ordered liberal visitation by the mother.[15,16]

In 1979, a decision of the highest court in New York affirming the termination of parental rights, the concept of *de facto* permanent neglect was attacked in a dissenting opinion as "cavalier readiness to drive parents out of a youngster's life."[17] In contrast, in the Probate Court a judge granted termination of parental rights saying, "At long last we see the legislature coming to grips with the basic conflict between parental and infants' rights. Too often a preoccupation with parental rights tends to blur the essential rights of an infant...(and bar the securing of) a permanent parental home."[18]

The personal convictions of judges led them to place different priorities in regard to the present rights of parents today and the future welfare of their children. Each month the *Juvenile Law Digest* reported divergent viewpoints. In one state, courts emphasized the importance of the psychological parent and terminated the rights of parents deemed unequal to the tasks of parenting. In another, parental rights were terminated only if the parent was found to be "truly psychotic." One court found the failure to pay a court order for support of a child in foster care a ground for termination. Some

courts were harsh with neglectful mothers, whereas others would not terminate parental rights unless the mother's immoral behavior "directly af-
fects the welfare of her children."

Judges also faced a variety of requirements under state statutes for terminating parental rights. Legislators, like judges sailed by different stars.
Some statutes allowed termination only if preceded by extensive efforts to
first improve the family situation.[19] Despite such a requirement, one court
held that every possible method for rehabilitating a mentally retarded
mother need not be exhausted, if the delay endangered the health and future
of a child.[20]

When the concept of terminating the rights of natural parents was still
novel, both judges and legislators faced opposition from some voluntary
agencies. For some agencies it was not only resistance to change that caused
opposition. Soon after the passage of the first permanent neglect statute,
counsel for one large group of sectarian agencies stated in open court that
compliance with the law would conflict with deeply held religious beliefs
on the rights of natural parents. He stated the agencies he represented would
never invoke the statute. After a period of time, this same lawyer and his
agencies came to see that to free children for adoption, when there was no
hope of return to natural parents, was indeed a blessing.

Even when the concept of terminating parental rights was written into
law and accepted verbally, freeing children for adoption continued to lag.
As late as 1972, an agency requested extension of foster care for two sisters,
ages 6 and 8, who had been in placement for 5 years. The mother had moved
to California 5 years earlier and had never visited the children. The father
had been certified as mentally ill. When asked by the court for an explanation as to why no petition had been brought to terminate parental rights, staff
offered a series of inconsistent explanations. The first was that the mother
was in California; the second, that the father had been certified as insane;
the third, that some correspondence from the mother suggested a "mixed
message" about her feelings for the children. The final excuse was that the
failure to act was due to a "discrepancy in the casework philosophy." It was
only after the court refused to extend placement that the agency worker acknowledged that the foster parents had wanted to adopt these two children
for the past 4 years.

The public Department of Social Services played a passive, if not an-
tagonistic, role when a judge challenged inaction by a child-care agency to
seek termination of parental rights for a child. The Department had been ac-

customed to paying the bill and leaving all else to the custodial agencies. It appeared satisfied with names, numbers and skimpy reports on children once placed in foster care. It seemed to fear that questioning what was done or left undone would open a Pandora's box. Similarly, State Board reports on foster care agencies did not question why children remained in care year after year.

Beyond and Before the Best Interest

The concept of permanent neglect, developed in 1959, and the slow advances toward greater permanence for children received a major shot in the arm in 1973. *Beyond the Best Interests of the Child*, a small volume by Anna Freud, together with Professor Joseph Goldstein and Dr. Albert Solnit, both of Yale, illumined and flooded the child care scene for a while.[21] It defined permanence for a child as a continuing relationship with one caring adult and contended that this should be the entitlement of every child. This work presented a broad challenge to child welfare and the Juvenile Court. A second volume published 6 years later by the same authors, however, stressed the increasingly popular theme that the integrity of the family must be protected, especially against intervention by the state.[22] It asked "What can justify overcoming the presumption in law that parents are free to determine what is best for their children in accord with their beliefs, preferences and life styles?"[23]

The latter position was seized on to approve survival in an "intact family," unless there was risk of serious bodily harm. Despite the professional background of the authors and their earlier emphasis on psychological parenting, emotional neglect was all but eliminated as sufficient reason for removal of a child by the state. At the same time, the authors proposed cutting all ties with natural parents where a child had been in foster care for a fixed period. Taken together, priority was to be given to the rights of parents so long as a child was within family walls, but priority was given to the rights of children when children were living outside family walls. They adopted the lower standard of "the least detrimental" alternative as a criterion for removal of children from their natural parents to replace the child's "best interest."[24,25]

Doctrine of Family Autonomy

The opposition to termination of parental rights was only one aspect of a more general thesis supporting family autonomy and freedom from state intervention. Public defenders of parents charged with long-term neglect demanded proof that removal of a child would cause less harm and do more good than leaving the child in the family. At times, defense counsel appeared more ardent than the parents in pressing for the return of the child to the natural parent. They believed they were serving a larger cause than the well-being of a single child.

In one Massachusetts case, the court granted permission for a child to be freed for adoption by loving foster parents who had had him since birth. The mother, encouraged by counsel, appealed to a series of State and Federal Courts. The result was that the foster parents gave up after 5 years of legal contests. Eventually, the child had to be placed with strangers for adoption when he was 8 years old and his right to be adopted had finally been established. In the words of the child's caseworker, "I certainly was able to grasp the abstract issues, but I deeply regret that the very real human beings most affected were overlooked."[26]

In Massachusetts, as in other states, counsel argued that the statute allowing freeing a child for adoption without parental consent was too vague, because it did not require a specific finding of parental "unfitness." The Massachusetts statute had, however, required the court to consider the ability, capacity, fitness, and readiness of the parent to "assume responsibility."[27]

Even some psychiatrists who treated mentally ill parents, but never saw their children, also proposed "one more chance" as medicine that might prove helpful to the parent. On such a recommendation, Tony, placed at birth, was released to his mentally ill mother, and returned to his foster home only after he was hospitalized for further serious injuries inflicted by the mother. Still, the agency was reluctant to file a petition to free Tony for adoption because the mother repeated her wish to hold on to him. When termination was ordered by the court, counsel for the agency remarked blandly that Tony would profit by the court's action, and thanked the court for its interest.

Voluntary child-care agencies and public defenders were not alone in resisting what they saw as a threat to family autonomy through the termination of parental rights. Nine national child welfare and advocacy groups filed a brief in a suit seeking review of a decision to terminate parental rights under the Delaware statute.[28] In accordance with the anti-interventionist mood of the 1970s, the brief began with the statement: "Americans have a deep conviction that the family must be preserved as the fundamental social unit in our society," and argued that the Supreme Court should lay down constitutionally adequate standards for termination of parental rights. This was the decade for rules and regulations in child care.

Claiming they did not know the facts of the case, these eminent child advocates distanced themselves from the children and concentrated on procedural questions. They ignored findings by the lower courts of tragic long-lasting parental neglect and the inability of the parents to provide a home. The parents were half-brother and sister, were not married to one another and were permanently separated. The mother had married another man and the father had left the state. The record of the father showed excessive drinking, a poor work record, and a conviction for "offensive touching" of his 3-year-old daughter. Ultimately in 1982, the United States Supreme Court dismissed the appeal from lower court decisions terminating parental rights.[29,30] In the intervening 2 years, Delaware had added statutory conditions for terminating parental rights, but there was little remaining likelihood that the children over whom the battle had been fought would ever have a permanent home.

The Search for Permanence: Limited by Discrimination and Distancing

The most deep-seated obstacle to securing a permanent alternative for children, however, arose from the failure of child welfare, the courts, and communities to seek and find homes for children most in need—nonwhite children, older children, handicapped, and emotionally troubled children. They were the castaways. It is only in the last few years that some groups like Adopt-A-Child have sought out these children and have tried to find homes for them.

Skepticism about what would be done for these children caused opposition to removal from families, even when children were subject to serious parental neglect. Counsel for children or parents challenged termination of parental rights and the testimony of psychiatrists on the forseeable future of mentally ill parents.

In other courts that heard custody battles between better circumstanced parents, increasing consideration was given to the wishes of children, to expert testimony on the emotional needs of children, and to the capacity of each parent to meet the needs of their children. In the Juvenile Court, such questions were rarely asked to aid the castaway children for whose custody no one battled. For poor and minority children, the standard for removal had been reduced to past, serious physical abuse and the threat of serious physical injury. Traditional discrimination and lack of services stayed the search for permanence.

Permanence for Children Today

General verbal agreement on the importance of a permanent home for every child has grown, but conflicts about how to achieve the goal remain. The values placed on natural families and fear of state intervention have caused legislatures to be reluctant and judges to procrastinate. The pulls and tugs are strong. When the federal government turned to legal experts for advice, a model draft act for termination of parental rights in the late 1970s was described as providing a "reasonable and clear ground for the rights and interests of both children and parents."[31,32] This theoretical boxing of the compass was not helpful when dealing with the lives of individual children or of their parents.

At the state level, efforts varied widely. In some states, comprehensive preventive programs were initiated. In others there were more admonitions about prevention of family break-up, than substantive aid to troubled parents or children. In still others, the principle of permanence was so joined with saving costs of foster care that a premature dumping process added further risks for neglected and abused children. Some were discharged to parents unable or reluctant to accept them. Others were prematurely discharged to adoptive homes for which they were not ready. The absence of follow-up studies on the consequences of discharges made it impossible to get the facts on the injuries or benefits for the children involved.

Despite all prejudices, fears, and errors, the search for greater permanence for all children has edged forward since 1959. The road to more effective prevention of family break-ups or injuries within the family is still rocky and uneven. But the untapped potential within human beings to reach out to children in need of permanent homes had been rediscovered by those ready to search for greater justice to all children.

Chapter 6
The Unmarried Mother, Illegitimacy, and Adoption

The road from sin to punishment has been strewn with unmarried mothers and their children. Mothers have been subjected to scorn and punishment, the children to condescension and rejection. Both have been punished by forced separation and by being tied to one another. They are rarely completely freed from one another emotionally. "Illegitimate" children and their mothers have been made hostage to one another.

Cruelty and self-righteousness as practiced in colonial America, vividly portrayed by Nathaniel Hawthorne in *The Scarlet Letter*, holds added meaning today. The 18th-century ministers who sat in public judgment on Hester Prynne, like Congress and state legislatures today, demanded that the unmarried mother identify the father as a condition to lessening her punishment. The eldest clergyman thundered: "Speak out the name. That and thy repentance may avail to take the scarlet letter off thy breast...." Fortunately for Hester Prynne, unlike unmarried mothers dependent on public assistance, she was not forced by a Federal Location Service to choose between identifying and prosecuting a missing father or having support for her child transferred to a third person.

Unmarried mothers, like Hester Prynne, have always been protected when they had independent means, or family members to defend them. In 1966, a father appealed from a Juvenile Court decision annulling the marriage of his 17-year-old pregnant daughter, and committing her to a State Training School. In vacating the commitment and reinstating the marriage, the Appellate Court noted that the girl's father was the owner of property and was willing to help the young couple.[1]

Political Attacks on Unmarried Mothers

Unmarried mothers, without independent means, have been a constant target for political attacks. They have been repeatedly charged by political leaders with having illegitimate babies in order to get more welfare. Relief has been described as a "bonus" for unmarried motherhood, although a Congressional Committee (informed by the Social Security Administration in 1966) reported that 87% of the children born out of wedlock were being supported by parents, adoptive parents, or relatives, and that only 13% were on welfare rolls. The Federal Social Security Administration noted that it would be surprising if mothers, who could receive only "part of the basic cost for rearing another child," would be moved to have more pregnancies to secure so little aid![2]

Ten years later the Federal Advisory Council on Public Assistance found it necessary to answer the same old charge and asked: "Does anyone believe that a woman in her right mind would have an illegitimate baby just to get an ADC payment of $20 to $30 a month?" The Council urged that the primary criterion for financial assistance to a needy child should be the child's need.

Nevertheless, attacks on mothers of illegitimate children continue. Proposals for checking illegitimacy have ranged from limiting help to the first child born out of wedlock, to total exclusion from ADC of all children born out of wedlock. In 1966, *The Saturday Evening Post* ran a major piece entitled "Are We Paying an Illegitimacy Bonus?" It repeated gossip about promiscuous women who conceived babies so as to live off the taxpayers, about unmarried mothers who hid their boyfriends, and about welfare workers "buffaloed by cheats." One mother in North Carolina, portrayed repeatedly in the press as refusing marriage while bearing more and more children so as to collect more ADC, was held up as an example. Investigation by the State Commissioner, Ellen Winston, uncovered that this mother was nonexistent. A statistical rebuttal of widespread fraud was presented by the Bureau of Public Assistance, placing fraudulent recipients of ADC at nine-tenths of 1% (.009).

Among other harassing devices, "midnight raids" were ordered to find hidden boyfriends. When legally challenged as unconstitutional, a representative of the Maryland State Board of Public Welfare sarcastically proposed, "We should now advise all women recipients that if they invite a man in, be sure to do so after 10 p.m."[3]

With such widespread suspicion, the appearance of the words "unmarried mother," (abbreviated "U.M."), or a child's court record with the initials "O.W." (for "out of wedlock") gave reason for anxiety. Would the words or the initials be pronounced aloud or whispered as though mother and child were nonpersons who would not hear or understand. Hostile attitudes toward unmarried mothers and their children were played out in many ways. The United States Supreme Court, the lower courts, state laws, and widespread prejudice all played a role in what happened to unmarried mothers and their children throughout the years.

Uncertain Justice in the Supreme Court

It was not until 1968 that the Supreme Court ruled that an illegitimate child could recover for the wrongful death of a mother.[4] The sole dissent, by Judge Rehnquist, expressed fear that this decision would tend to encourage immorality. When the Supreme Court in that same year upheld legislative discrimination against an illegitimate child, Justice Douglas dissented:

> Illegitimate children are not non-persons. ... They are humans, live and have their being. They are clearly "persons" within the meaning of the Equal Protection Clause of the Fourteenth Amendment."[5,6]

The Supreme Court zig-zagged in its protection of illegitimate children. In 1967, it invalidated a 1964 Alabama statute that denied AFDC to a child if the mother cohabited in or outside the home with an able-bodied man. The state law was held inconsistent with the Social Security Act and in violation of the Equal Protection Clause of the Constitution.[7] In 1977, the Supreme Court struck down an Illinois statute that allowed illegitimate children to inherit only from their mothers but not from fathers who died "intestate." But in this 5–4 decision, the court also placed illegitimate children in a separate and inferior category as compared to children born in wedlock.[8] On the same day, the Supreme Court also upheld a discriminatory provision in the Immigration Law that denied preference for permanent residence to the illegitimate children of U.S. citizens.[9]

In 1979, the Supreme Court rejected an equal protection challenge when it granted benefits to the widow of a deceased wage earner but denied them to his illegitimate child. Justice Rehnquist, writing for the 5-4 majority, held that the Social Security provisions were intended to benefit spouses and not children.[10] This position contradicted earlier decisions holding that the Act was intended to permit women to "devote themselves to the care of their children."

In the 1980s, the majority of the Supreme Court sustained the Hyde Amendment, denying Medicaid to poor women seeking abortions. In his dissent, Justice Brennan wrote that the majority opinion reminded him of the words of Anatole France, that "the law, in its majestic quality, forbids the rich as well as the poor to sleep under the bridges, to beg in the street and to steal bread."

Harassment by State Legislature

Some state legislatures had introduced new harassments against unmarried mothers and their children. Connecticut led the way. Despite its liberal history in many other areas of law and social welfare, it engaged in three successive attempts to threaten the support and care of illegitimate children. Two legislative devices cut off benefits to children or reduced family budgets if mothers failed to identify and prosecute absent fathers. After these legislative efforts were struck down as in conflict with the Social Security Act,[11] Connecticut enacted a statute ordering mothers to identify the absent father, or be subjected to a fine or imprisonment for up to 1 year.[12]

Although the legislative language did not restrict such actions to mothers who received ADC, actions were brought only against mothers receiving public assistance. This law did not allow exceptions for good cause, stating that, "The mother of any child for whom adjudication of paternity is sought shall not be excused from testifying because her evidence may tend to disgrace or incriminate her."

One mother testified that the father was a drug addict, had been convicted of criminal conduct, and that a fugitive warrant had been issued for his arrest. She expressed great fear for herself and her child if she identified the father and he was brought to court. The judge replied he had no discretion to consider her reasons and was only presiding to enforce "the law." He gave the mother 1 week to comply or be prepared for incarceration. When counsel asked what would happen if the mother could not make arrangements for care of her infant, the judge replied, "That is her problem."[13]

Other judges also ruled they had no power to consider the mother's reasons for refusal to obey the statute. A bit of male chauvinism in the State's brief supporting the Connecticut statute must have read like gallows humor to unmarried mothers, threatened with incarceration for not identifying fathers who had never acknowledged or supported their infants: "The status of legitimacy, or of having knowledge and proof of one's paternity ... means for example that when ... any of the myriad forms that we fill out in our daily lives is filled out by an illegitimate child, he can fill in the blanks pertaining to 'Father.' ... There exists ... the valuable status of being the child of an individual male...." The District Court upheld this statute stating, "While incarceration of contemptuous mothers may not always be in the child's best interest, this does not establish an unreasonable conflict between the two...." On appeal to the Supreme Court on behalf of mothers threatened with imprisonment, 27 national organizations in child care, mental health, family welfare, and children's rights filed an *amicus* brief challenging the constitutionality of the Connecticut Act.[14] The brief pointed out that the incarceration of the unmarried mothers would make orphans of illegitimate children by depriving them of their only known and concerned parent. While the appeal was pending, Congress amended the Social Security Act to impose penalties on any state that failed to force mothers on AFDC to identify and to prosecute absent fathers. Popularly known as the "Drag or Dad" law, one aspect of the law did drag behind—the working out of what should be allowed as "good cause for exceptions" for mothers who refused cooperation.

The Supreme Court did not hold the Connecticut statute was unconstitutional. However, it dismissed the appeal with direction that the lower court review its procedures in the light of the new Social Security Amendment, which included no threats of imprisonment against the mothers. This ended the criminal proceedings against mothers in Connecticut, but national and state location services became larger and larger bureaucracies.

Like so many earlier forms of harassment, coercive action against unmarried mothers disguised the primary fiscal interest with expressions of concern for children. State legislatures and administrative agencies maintained that their concern was with the child's right to future financial support, even when a father was a confirmed drug addict, had been sentenced to long-term imprisonment, or was immune from a finding of paternity and the duty of support by reason of the passage of time. The fiscal benefits to the state and Federal governments have been substantial.

Exploitation and Discrimination by Social Agencies and Schools

For unmarried women without support, exploitation added further insult and injury. In 1938, when a girl who had decided to keep her baby did not appear for a hearing, I learned that she had been detained by the "charitable" hospital where the infant had been born. Its rules required her to work 3 months and 21 days after confinement before being allowed to take her baby home. When questioned, the hospital claimed its practice was by arrangement with the Department of Welfare. This 15-year-old, after delivering her baby, had been assigned to scrub up the postoperative room from 7 p.m. to 7 a.m. each night. The hospital explained that the work requirement was to help the young mother learn how to care for her baby. But, in fact, she was allowed only a 1-hour daily visit with her child, with no opportunity to feed or bathe her infant.[15]

Unmarried mothers were required by some social agencies to care for their babies until they were found healthy, attractive, and ready for adoptive placement. That this practice made separation and surrender more painful for the mother and her infant was disregarded or seen as appropriate punishment. A similar attitude toward unmarried mothers allowed over-zealous hospital, welfare, and court personnel to impose religious identification on a child born out of wedlock regardless of the mother's wishes. As late as the 1970s, the public department in New York did not permit an unmarried mother to say that she only wanted the best adoptive home for her child, regardless of religion. The one exception was for children of interracial backgrounds for whom the Department of Welfare expected difficulty in finding an adoptive home.[16]

It was not only social agencies and the Welfare Department that exercised heavy-handed control over unmarried, pregnant girls. If they were returned home by the court, schools excluded them with the description of "medical suspensions." It was not until the late 1960s that they were admitted to special schools, and it was a decade later before they were permitted to return to their regular schools. If these girls could not return home and were not accepted by a voluntary agency for care, an institution for delinquents was the only resource available to the court.

As the years passed and more unmarried girls decided to keep their babies, aid fell far short of what mothers and children needed. If the girl was under 18, she was not entitled to public assistance to establish a household for herself and her baby, no matter how inadequate or inhospitable her family home might be. When she became 18, the public assistance allowed was insufficient to provide more than a furnished room. No funds were granted for respite from 24-hour responsibility for her baby. Few group or foster home settings were available to help her live with and care for her baby. There was little assistance to help her return to school or to get the training needed to become independent.

Responses to an article on illegitimacy I wrote for the *Woman's Home Companion* in 1947 resulted in a deluge of mail including both attacks on my lack of morality and praise for my "courage." One letter from a Mormon elder concluded that I had missed the only true solution: "It is strange that one possessed of such boldness and intelligence can walk so near the river of life and not see it.... Plural wives solve all the problems you pose and it is the only marriage method that does solve all the problems..." In a far different vein, a woman wrote, "If women cannot have motherhood in safety they are nothing....Paternity cases should be stopped...I know from experience that during the suit the baby is called dirty names and the mother is obliged to degrade herself by relating her most intimate actions. Even if more than a few paltry dollars were at stake, this would not be fair. Establishing paternity is not, cannot be worth such degradation, and in public, too. To rate as a father, a man should be willing to declare it of his own accord."

The "Illegitimate Child"

Even if the Supreme Court had affirmed that legitimate and illegitimate children are legal equals, the gulf between the abstract principle of equality and meaningful implementation would have loomed wide.[17]

Soon after I went on the bench, I witnessed how prejudice and venom could strike at a child born out of wedlock. A buxom teacher appeared against a 12-year-old boy. With angry gestures, she described how she had watched from a window in the school, as he cut the rear tires on her car. I asked if this was true, and the boy hung his head and was silent. When I asked why he had done it, the words poured out: "I stepped out of line. She yelled at me. She shouted, 'What's your name, if you have a name?'" Then he put his head in his hands and sobbed. The words of this teacher had struck deeply at a boy who had never known his father.

Discrimination and injury took many forms in private and public actions against children conceived or born out of wedlock. At an international conference on adoption some years ago, a representative from one Middle Eastern country proudly announced that her country had no children for adoption. When privately asked how this could be, the worker explained that if an unmarried woman became pregnant she had to get rid of the unborn infant or face death at the hands of her male relatives so that they would not be disgraced. In other lands, ostracism of the child, a lifetime of begging, and continuing hurts have taken many forms.

In the United States, prejudice and discrimination against illegitimate children was written into many state laws. Begetting an illegitimate child was treated as a minor offense of the father—a misdemeanor or a petty misdemeanor.[18] In Louisiana, the code (until 1952) declared that "natural fathers and mothers can, in no case, dispose of property in favor of their adulterous or incestuous children," except for necessary sustenance or to make them self-supporting. Some states have been satisfied with verbal reforms. Thus, New York substituted "out of wedlock" for "illegitimate" in 1925, "natural" for "out of wedlock" in 1930, and prohibited the use of the words "bastard" or "illegitimate" in public documents or proceedings in 1947. Substantive changes in the state laws and equal treatment of illegitimate children came more slowly. In 1940, only 18 states allowed changes in birth certificates to obliterate the mark of illegitimacy, even when a child had been legitimized by marriage of the parents.[19]

In 1925, Arizona was alone in enacting legislation declaring that a child born out of wedlock was the legitimate child of both parents. Other states failed to follow, and in 1979 only one more state, Oregon, had passed legislation that illegitimacy was nonexistent. Probably most immediately harmful to many illegitimate children, legislative standards for support reduced them to second-class children. For them, the standards for support required by law were often limited to necessities, continued for fewer years than for legitimate children, and were not based on the means of their fathers.

When paternity cases were transferred in New York from the Criminal Court to the Family Court in 1962, I saw how the double standard affected children. Hearings were held in a cavernous, decrepit, and filthy building adjacent to the Criminal Court. The halls swarmed with "runners," lawyers seeking to pick up and defend putative fathers for small fees. A backlog of

18,000 cases existed. There were no intake workers to interview mothers, and the probation officers were of low caliber. No representatives of voluntary agencies were present in this dismal setting to aid or even speak to unmarried mothers. Mothers were often not notified of the hearings, which were repeatedly adjourned. City attorneys were assigned to represent unmarried mothers, without their knowledge or consent, on the theory that all children born out of wedlock and their mothers were or would become public charges. When men acknowledged paternity, these attorneys were quick to accept inadequate offers for child support, because whatever was paid would reduce the welfare payments. Without consent of the mother, child support was made payable to the Department of Welfare as an offset against present or future public assistance. With comparable disregard for the wishes of the mothers or the well-being of the children, city counsel approved visitation by the father, if requested, whenever a father agreed to contribute.

In Family Court, when fathers requested visitation, decisions were also too often casual or mercurial. Assumed to be a bird of passage, unmarried fathers were denied visitation by some judges. Other judges granted visitation as a *quid pro quo* for support with little regard for the consequences to the child or mother. Although the transfer of jurisdiction from the Criminal Court produced improvements, including the elimination of runners and the provision for notice to mothers, the low standard for support fixed by legislation for the illegitimate child was continued.

Increased concern for the rights of women failed to challenge the inferior treatment of children born out of wedlock or of their mothers. The old assumption continued that custody of an illegitimate child automatically went to the mother, like a burden or benefit running with the land. No duty was imposed on fathers to contribute to mothers caring for their children born out of wedlock. That unmarried mothers who provide care for their children born out of wedlock are not entitled to any support from the fathers goes largely unchallenged. This treatment is supported by the present policy that an unmarried mother is entitled to public assistance only while her child is below school age. Today there is growing demand that mothers dependent on welfare should go to work while their children are still infants or preschool children.

The inequities, neglect, and punishments imposed on unmarried mothers and their children have become intensified with the dramatic rise of the single-parent family. The 21% of children who lived with a single parent in 1983 is expected to rise to 25% by 1990.[20] This increase is attributed to many causes, such as looser morality, more divorces, later marriages, changes in sexual mores, and the employment of more women outside their homes. The cost to taxpayers and the poverty of the single-parent family is bewailed. Far less concern is shown for the consequences to mothers and children when fiscal restraints deprive them of prenatal care that results in low birth weights and other complications that could be prevented. The disproportionate rise of single black parents has produced anger but little confrontation with racial discrimination as a major cause of single parenthood (see chapter 10).

For the poor, the sentiments of Bonar Thompson go to the essence of how children born out of wedlock are treated if they need aid: "My birth was a *faux pas*, the tragedy not of being born out of *wedlock*, but having been born out of *pocket*."[21]

Adoption: From Elitism to Outreach

Out of the contradictory treatment accorded to a few high-born bastards and the neglect of countless illegitimate children, adoption struggled to be born. Despite the biblical tale of Moses and the princess, adoption was denied legal status in this country until the mid-19th century.[22] In a 1963 probation memorandum to New York judges, adoption was still described as a "privilege rather than a right," with the reminder that "what is not found in the statutes is for the legislature to supply and not for the court to do."

Such a pronouncement seemed especially grating to me because adoption had been a household word since my childhood. My mother learned in 1916 that there were Protestant and Catholic agencies in New York to place children in adoptive homes, but that there was only one orphanage for homeless Jewish children. Shocked, she secured a list of Jewish children who were free to be adopted. When I was 13, she took me with her to visit the big orphanage in Manhattan for Jewish children.

We were ushered into the director's office and received with formal courtesy until my mother presented the list and asked to see the children. When a little girl of about 5 or 6 wandered into the office, my mother asked in a whisper whether she was free for adoption. A rough, loud answer came, "You want even a common little thief?" My only other recollection of that visit is of walking from the director's office into a large room, where small children surrounded us and begged, "Will you be my mommie?" From that day on for months, my father never knew whether his bed would be occupied by a child my mother brought home until she could find an adoptive family. One little girl arrived in a shabby dress and I helped bathe her. Her carrot-colored hair seemed to turn to gold. Then she was dressed in a Liberty frock and taken downstairs to meet prospective parents. There was also a dark-haired little boy whose eyes, like my father's, were slightly crossed. My brother and I agreed secretly that he looked like our father.

From this unprofessional start an agency grew and placed thousands of children in adoptive homes. Today it is nonsectarian and cares for children regardless of race, religion, or national origin. It is now finding homes for children from Vietnam, Cambodia, and Haiti, as well as for American children of all races.[23]

Adoption long functioned in elitist agencies—separated from other child-care services and treated as superior by reason of the class of adoptive families. Adoption agencies bestowed benefits on well-to-do, childless families and received gratitude and gifts in return. They provided healthy, white infants and assured adoptive parents that the children were untainted by a family background of mental illness or crime. They assumed the miraculous ability to select which child should be placed with which family. Adoptive families were studied (with politesse) in depth not accorded to foster families. Separated by religion, adoption agencies were also insulated from the general problems of poor children. They long remained aloof from the needs of nonwhite children and families.

Racial prejudice also appeared in court decisions that disapproved adoptions of black children by long-term white foster parents and of white children by long-term black foster parents. In the 1960s, racial prejudice surfaced in a new way. Numbers of white, pregnant college students surrendered their newborn babies for adoption. They repeatedly told of rape by a black or that their pregnancies resulted from short affairs with a black fellow student. When many of their babies appeared white, agencies were baffled as to whether they should be placed with white or black families. Fearful of "throwbacks" to blackness, they consulted the distinguished anthropologist, Dr. Harry Shapiro. He replied that if all the black characteristics were recessive at 6 months of age, a child born to the adopted child could be no darker than the darker of the two parents. This encouraged adoption agencies to place infants without black characteristics in white families.

The Scarcity of White Babies for Adoption

As birth control and abortions reduced the supply of white babies for adoption, the gray and black markets multiplied. The gray market was not-for-profit. One obstetrician proudly stated, "In one hospital room I had a sad young couple whose baby had died. In another room, I had an unmarried teenager who did not want to keep her healthy baby. So I just moved that baby from one room to the other. Everyone was happy. Why should anyone object?" The black market was different. Families determined to adopt a child bought them from lawyers and intermediaries at increasing prices. In this period of scarcity of white adoptable children, a few agencies began to change former policies and placed children across racial lines. Old theories about the importance of "matching" physical characteristics of adopted children to those of their adoptive parents went out of style. It became more acceptable and even chic to adopt different-looking children, especially if they came from far-distant lands. Preference is still shown for Korean, Vietnamese, and Cambodian children, as against the many black children born in this country who are waiting for adoptive families. Traditional adoption had never reached more than a small number of children in need of permanent homes, although some social workers and agencies made valliant efforts. Nearly 40 years ago Florence Kreech, the director of Louise Wise Services, disbanded a unit for "unadoptable children," redefining "unadoptable" as those children for whom adoptive homes had not yet been found.

Today there is promise from the growing concensus in child welfare, in Congress, and in many state legislatures that every child is entitled to a permanent home. Yet, practice falls far short of that promise for children with physical, mental, or emotional handicaps. Most important, American nonwhite children wait in large numbers and outgrow the likelihood of ever being adopted. Progress has been slow, stymied by old prejudices.

It was not until 1982 that the first National Exchange was established to share information about children waiting for adoptive families. Even the Model Adoption Act of 1980, passed with the approval of child-welfare experts, clings to the concept that not only birth parents but that *any* blood relative should be given preference in the scarch for a home. It allows subsidies for adoptive families only after every effort has been made to find appropriate family members who will not need a subsidy. A blood relationship and reduced costs rather than the best hope for a child are thus still joined in adoptive policies and practices.

The Changing Role of Foster Parents

As I write, a childhood memory, perhaps exaggerated, returns. I was taken by my mother in a chauffeured limousine to visit a child "readied" for adoptive placement. The woman in the car was beautiful and elegantly dressed. Her long, white kid gloves, with many buttons, fascinated me on that warm spring day. Her husband tried hard to please her, as she reclined against a cushion, remote and silent. When the car stopped in front of a simple house in the suburbs, we all climbed the porch steps. In the doorway, a woman held up a small baby for inspection with tenderness and pride. Everyone looked at the baby as an adoptive prospect, nodded and returned to the car. Hardly a word was spoken to the foster mother, who still held the baby.

Foster parents were long treated as unskilled help. They received a pittance for the room and board of a child with nothing for their service. Responsible for the children 24 hours a day and 7 days a week, what they came to mean to the children in their care and what the children meant to them was disregarded. Some states required foster parents to sign agreements that they would never seek to adopt a foster child.

When a foster home couple resisted removal of a child, the child-care agency that had placed the child claimed absolute control. In court, the agency contended that foster parents should not become emotionally involved with children placed in their care. It argued that it was the duty of foster parents to provide a "neutral" atmosphere and the New York Court of Appeals accepted this position.[24]

The distancing of foster parents, like the distancing of neglected children, was made easier because both were rarely seen by judges. Judges generally received only written requests for longer stays in hospitals, shelters, institutions, or foster care. They were spared seeing lines of cribs holding listless babies or observing overworked staff in institutions that had too little time to pick up, to feed, or to cuddle an infant. When judges were advised that long-term care had been found for a child, they were satisfied and relieved by the submission of orders authorizing public reimbursement for long-term foster care.

In New York, the role of the foster parent began to change in 1962, when the Family Court was given the duty to review all cases of children in placement more than 18 months. By 1973, 24 states provided subsidies to foster home parents who adopted "hard-to-place" children. Foster home parents had come to be seen as an important resource for adoption as well as for foster home care. In 1979, Professor Fanshel reported that 72% of foster parents interviewed reacted favorably when asked about their interest in adoption.[25] A year later, Congress enacted the Federal Adoption Assistance and Child Welfare Act, requiring states to establish subsidy systems in order to encourage adoptions of children with special needs.[26]

Foster parents were the only adults who gave continuity of care to many thousands of children. Foster parents had provided the mainstay for permanence to children excluded from adoption because of individual problems, lack of services, or racial discrimination. Yet, foster parents were late in becoming articulate in regard to their rights. Finally, support for foster parent adoptions came from groups whose primary interest was to diminish the cost of foster care.

As in other reforms, converts to the right of permanence for children oversimplified what needed to be done without sufficient regard to the problems of individual children. Many demanded speedy discharge to the natural family or adoption by the foster family as the only alternatives. For some children accepting even loved foster parents as their parents in name is not tolerable. Adolescents, long in foster care, have special problems about adoption. Children with memories or fantasies about their birth parents could not forsake them. Such problems cannot be worked out by fiat, however well intentioned. Neither foster parents nor children should be coerced by the carrot of continuing subsidy or the stick of threatened removal of a child who is doing well in a foster home.

Over the years, foster parents have been whipsawed from opposite directions. For decades they were taken for granted and excluded from adopting children in their care. More recently, foster parents have been made the whipping boys by reformers bent on rescuing children from "the limbo of foster care." Winning balanced understanding and respect for foster parents, and their potential as long-term foster or adoptive parents, is still in the making.

New Rights for Adoptees and for Unmarried Fathers

Adoption agencies were shaken in the 1970s when a small group of adult adoptees demanded that "confidential" agency records about their natural parents and their adoptive parents be opened for their inspection. Following the "search for roots" in the black community, these white adoptees asserted the right to discover their true identity. They also asserted their right to meet their birth parents. When this position was publicized, many young adoptees appeared at the agencies through which they had been placed, asking to know more.

Most adoptees wanted information about their background, and only a small number wanted to meet their biological parents. This was also true in European countries where adoption records were open for inspection. Following extensive litigation, the Federal Courts sustained the New York statute that held adoption records confidential, but allowed their opening by a judge in individual cases for "good cause."[27]

The lower Federal Court had expressed concern for the privacy of biological parents, for the security of adoptive parents, and for the public's interest in the adoptive process. The decision to protect all three concerns was upheld by the Supreme Court.

Although the battles by organizations of adult adoptees for their right to information was widely publicized, legislative, judicial, and community attitudes also changed to enlarge the rights of unmarried fathers. Descriptive words moved from "putative" to "natural" to "birth" father. Decisions on visitation were broadened to allow shared or even sole custody to unmarried fathers. The rights of unmarried fathers moved ahead at a comparatively rapid pace.

In a path-breaking decision, the United States Supreme Court held that the denial of custody to an unmarried father, without due process, after the death of the mother, violated the father's constitutional rights.[28] Some state legislatures and lower courts went further, requiring notice to the unmarried father as a condition to the surrender of a child for adoption by the mother even when the alleged father had not acknowledged paternity or supported the child.

It has long been assumed that a roll in the hay was responsible for babies born out of wedlock, and that most of the fathers disappeared after a night's adventure. Recently, however, more workers in schools and adoption agencies are reporting that poor, adolescent parents have frequently known each other well, want to continue their relationship, and often hope to marry when it becomes possible. Some of the youths and their family members, give support for the child in ways characteristic of the extended family, although their own poverty and social disapproval have deterred such mutual financial aid. It is nearly 40 years since Maude Morlock, a renowned social worker, wrote that in Sweden, where attitudes toward out of wedlock mothers were less judgmental, 90% of the fathers acknowledged paternity.[29]

Adoption: Still in Flux

During the past 50 years, adoption moved beyond the highly selective placement of healthy, attractive, white infants in upper class childless families. It still has far to go. But under law, adoption in the United States has existed for little more than 100 years. During this time it has occupied a small but growing role in the world of child welfare beyond its numerical dimensions. It has reflected both old prejudices and new ideals of permanence for more children as it emerged from a tightly framed cocoon.

As this country faces vast changes in social mores, the marriage rate, the divorce rate, and the steady increase in single parents, adoption can be seen as one major way of providing permanency for more children. But, alone, it cannot achieve equal or adequate treatment for all children who could benefit from adoption. Real progress toward this goal will depend on far wider respect and support from the larger community for unmarried parents and their children.

Chapter 7
Sex and the Double Standard

On my first visit to the court in the mid-1930s, I saw how a Juvenile Court judge could enforce his personal sense of sexual morality. The mother and father were charged with impairing the morals of their three children. Not married, they were living in what the law then called a "common-law relationship." The parents, poor and foreign-born, stood with heads bowed during a long lecture on their behavior. At the end of his sermon, the judge announced that he would give the parents 10 days to get married before he decided whether to remove their children. In those days, when adultery was the only ground for divorce in New York, the judge did not ask whether the parents were free to marry, about their life together, let alone whether they wished to marry. Dismissed temporarily, the parents left without speaking a word. The man never returned to court. He disappeared, and the mother with her three children became one more family dependent on welfare.

The Court as Arbiter of "Morality"

A short time after my appointment to the bench, a neglect petition was brought charging that a mother was living with a man to whom she was not married. Her husband had deserted when the child was an infant, but that was not ground for divorce in those days. The man with whom she and her 8-year-old child lived had provided a good home for them all. He treated the child as his own and the child regarded him as her father. In the neighborhood they were known as husband and wife. There was no charge of promiscuity and the parties regarded their relationship as a marriage.

With no evidence of neglect, I dismissed the petition. The Big Sisters of the mother's faith "respectfully" requested a conference in chambers. They expressed dismay over my action. I spoke of the care and love the child was receiving from her mother and her "stepfather." I spoke of the injury that would result from the removal of the child's second father or the removal of the child from the only home she had ever known. My visitors remained unmoved, and one Big Sister finally asked, in sepulchral tones, whether I was not "condoning adultery."

The rumor quickly spread that I was anti-Catholic. My action to protect a Catholic child was not noted. Such zealous guarding of morality made judges and staff cautious. A cloak of silence among judges prevented honest discussion of differences in viewpoint on religious issues.

Three small children—ages 6, 8, and 9—whose mother had died were brought to court as neglected because they were living with their father and a woman to whom he was not married. Investigation showed that this was a happy home and that the woman and children were devoted to one another. Moving cautiously, I paroled them back to the home despite obvious signs of disapproval from staff and a sectarian agency. A year later, when the storm and interest had passed, the probation officer reported that all was going well, and I felt the case could be dismissed.

A similar confrontation arose when 15-year-old Jerome was ordered to leave his father's home because the father was living with a woman to whom he was not married. The mother had refused a divorce on religious grounds. After the boy ran away from her and returned to the father in violation of the order of a previous judge, the mother agreed to a divorce. She appeared in court to say that her son should be allowed to live with his father and "the other woman," who was making a good home for him. The judge addressed the probation officer who had filed the violation, "My feeling is that in this matter, our primary responsibility is to the child, though you did what you had to do.... We have to go beneath the surface violation and try to independently reach a fair conclusion as to whether this home is the best place." On a favorable probation report of the boy's progress after his return to the father, the judge discharged the boy to his father before the completion of the divorce action. Both the judge and the probation officer knew that another judge might reverse the decision to leave the boy in an "adulterous home."

Among the obstacles to justice, none was more rigid or fearsome than the "morality" expected in judicial decisions. This expectation of "morality" also required harsh disapproval of and punishments for children who had been sexually active. Judges, who had reached the bench through the rough and tumble of political clubs, treated sexual innocence as the most precious attribute of childhood. Once sullied by sexual experience, the child ceased, in their eyes, to be a child. Even a child sexually abused by an adult was separated from other children. Children who were the victims of sexual abuse were still placed in detention with delinquents, while the accused adults were released on bail by the Criminal Courts. It was as though removal of the bloom of "natural innocence" made the child delinquent.

Maria, aged 12, was charged with delinquency for "submitting to carnal abuse" by her 53-year-old stepfather. In the detention home, she was described as a petite, attractive little girl of normal intelligence, looking much younger than her age. Two years later (1956) the agency for delinquent girls to which she had been committed by the court alleged she was too difficult to handle. Despite feeling unloved, she begged to go home, if only her stepfather was removed. This her mother refused, fearing to lose her husband, the family breadwinner. The child was continued in placement as a delinquent.

Joetta, not yet 12, sexually assaulted by her stepfather during her first menstrual period, was terrified. She ran to the police for help. Taken to the Children's Court by the police, she was found neglected and so disturbed that she was sent to Bellevue Hospital. Having had "sexual experience" the court could only find placement for this child in an institution for older delinquents. After some time she was returned to Bellevue by the institution because of her "obscene language." Dr. Lauretta Bender, a leading child psychiatrist, found Joetta frightened and bitter, feeling she had been punished for something not her fault. Dr. Bender wrote: "At no point in her experience does it appear that anyone had made an effort to understand and explain to Joetta the significance of her experience or to contribute in any way to her except in a painful, punitive and derogatory fashion.... Whatever obscene language she used in the Home was used as a child uses it...only as a weapon against a situation which she found hard to accept."[1]

Many residential agencies rejected children who had had any sexual experience for either institutional or foster home care. One 10-year-old boy was brought before the court on a neglect petition against a stepmother of the Grimm's fairytale variety. She had mistreated him for years and had recently starved him for 1 week when he "talked back" to her. After referral for foster home care, the stepmother told the agency that, on one occasion, the 10-year-old had engaged in sex play with another child. All doors to foster home care were abruptly closed. The need to conceal sexual experience made it all the more shameful when the child and the court were found to have kept the "secret" in order to secure care from a "charitable" agency.

For a while, even a few clinicians rejected sexually active children and parents for treatment services. They devised the term *primitive social behavior* to describe these clients, especially if they were newcomers to New York or were nonwhite. They incorporated an old message that the poor should be neither "bad" nor "glad."

Within the court, rescue came from those clinicians, probation officers, and judges who rebelled against the harsh attitudes and exclusion from services of children who had known sex. They conspired to circumvent the mistreatment or nontreatment of these children. Some probation officers cleaned up records and adjourned cases until they could get before a sympathetic judge. They and cooperative members of the clinic staff would share material on a child's exposure to sex, forced incest, or sexual choices and advise a judge in chambers whether the child should be placed as neglected or delinquent or remain at home. Although such sharing contacts became more frequent with the passage of time and the growth of mutual confidence, there was always the uncomfortable sense that Big Brother was watching.

Homosexuality

Homosexuality was long treated in the court as nonexistent and beyond understanding. Like the ultimate punishment in Mennonite communities, a child who engaged in such activity was automatically excluded from contact with "unspoiled children" and found fit only for exile. When a judge complained in the 1950s that a homosexual incident had occurred in a public detention center, a committee of judges was officially appointed to investigate. We read studies reporting that nearly 40% of the total male population had some homosexual experience during their lives, and that such experiences were frequent in single-sex group-living situations. One of the judges was aghast. Deeply religious and a passionate devotee of outdoor sports, he regarded homosexuality with such horror that he could not bring himself to sign the majority report that discussed homosexuality objectively. Also, being an honest man, he never submitted a dissenting report.

Incest

Seduction, rape, or sexual intimacy between a father and daughter was the one unforgivable crime that was met with disbelief and abhorrence in the Juvenile Court. These cases, still few in number, were baffling to judges. They saw their duty as limited to removing the girl to some safe place until the "bad" parent moved away or was removed from the home by the Criminal Court.

A complete turnabout appeared during the 1970s. At that time, some sociologists and public defenders questioned the removal of a girl who had experienced incest unless the court could find that removal from the home would be less harmful to her than leaving her in the home. Counsel contended that there was no proof that serious harm resulted from sexual relations within the home in the absence of physical injury. They contended that the discovery of incest would be a safeguard against repetition and questioned the value of treatment outside the home. These anti-interventionist positions were widely adopted by some professional groups for a time.[2]

Opposition to this position was presented by two pioneers in child abuse, Dr. Ruth Kempe and Dr. Henry Kempe. They took the position that "the failure to treat the victim is a far more serious societal deficiency than failure to punish the perpetrators."[3] Having spent years working directly with abused children, they could not accept the overoptimistic expectations of theorists for children who had been "exposed to dangerous developmental crippling." As more has been learned about incest within families and its resulting scars, the admonitions that it be overlooked have been slowly muted.

Sexism and the Double Standard for Girls

Philosophically, ancient China had seen the world as the product of two interacting, complementary elements, Yin and Yang. Yin was the attribute of all things male, bright, strong, and active. Under Confucian teaching, "a wife striking her husband deserved one hundred blows, whereas a husband striking his wife was punishable only if she was badly injured and lodged a complaint."[4] Rulers of ancient and modern times have shown little sympathy toward women or girls who violated the law. Yet, in the third century B.C., a Buddhist emperor in India ordered the release of women prisoners who had children. Twenty-two centuries later, President Francois

Mitterand, in granting clemency to a number of women prisoners in France, expressed concern that their children were suffering social and psychological problems.[5] These were exceptions. Consistent with age-old and world-wide traditions, female prisoners and delinquent girls in the United States have been subjected to punishment with lesser services for education, training, recreation, and return to the community than their male counterparts.

In the Juvenile Court, girls charged with sexual misconduct were seen as dark birds. With romantic notions about the natural moral superiority of females, discomfort with sexually active girls caused them to be seen as unlikable, if not repulsive. The low proportion of delinquent girls compared to delinquent boys (less than 1:4) nurtured ongoing expectations of higher female morality and invited stricter punishment when females failed to behave "properly."

Similar attitudes and expectations for daughters moved parents to turn to the courts for corrective action, when girls truanted, stayed out late, drank, or engaged in sex. Having done so, they were reluctant to take their daughters home, and often asked that they be taught a lesson by being put away and out of danger. Girls felt forced to accept such parental responses to sexual experience. Fifteen-year-old Naomi was sent to detention to prevent further contact with the young man she hoped to marry. Detention staff noted her excellent adjustment, and her "understanding that she is unable to return home because of parental opposition."[6]

Judges, too, were more anxious about paroling girls before deciding on probation or placement. They feared that if a girl got into "trouble" while on parole, the parents would blame them. In the Criminal Courts, girls over 16 were less likely than boys to be paroled or granted bail. In explanation one judge announced, "I don't give bail to prostitutes. They change their names and addresses too easily."

Juvenile Court judges had little latitude in the placement of delinquent, adolescent girls. Few voluntary agencies accepted them. The only one that accepted Protestant, black girls in New York City closed in the 1940s for lack of funds. All black, delinquent girls had to be sent to the State Training School or to one of a few Catholic institutions that would accept them. The State Training School rejected pregnant girls, claiming it was "not possible to carry out a program in which pregnant girls can participate."

On judicial visits to voluntary institutions for delinquent girls, one saw no overt cruelty. But, for the most part, they were dismal places for adolescents. Large dormitories held narrow beds in row on row. There was little furniture and there were no pictures or play spaces to relieve the somber, barrack-like rooms. Specific duties were assigned to each girl with detailed schedules for cleaning, laundry, kitchen work, and endless mopping and shining of floors. The charter of one agency, adopted in 1869, still in force in 1943, stated its mission to be "the redemption and reclamation of females who have been allured from the path of virtue." Although the maintenance work required of the girls reduced the cost of their care, no programs were provided to educate them or to train them for other work. The girls were silent—furtively raising their eyes when visitors came. These institutions had been intended as places for penance, and they continued as such for many decades.

Sexual activity resulting in pregnancy frequently led to institutional placement to prevent family disgrace more than to protect the girl. In the absence of forcible rape, the sexual activity of boys responsible for the pregnancies were all but taken for granted as "normal," and no action was taken against the boys. So long as a girl "allowed sex," she was held responsible for the consequences.

Judicial and Legislative Discrimination

In the Family Court, discriminatory treatment against females was not limited to the girls. Mothers were treated differently than fathers. Contradictory positions were expressed about the mother's duty to stay at home with her children or to work in order to aid in their support. Idealization of the woman's role imposed more exacting demands on mothers than on fathers, who were assumed to be the breadwinners. When parents were living separately, after determining the amount of paternal support, judges would ask the fathers what visitation they wanted with their children. Fixed by the court, such visitation was treated as a permanent privilege without any obligation that the father use it. Only default in support payments or physical abuse by the father provided grounds for further court action by the mother.

Discrimination against girls and women was not unique to the Family Court. State legislatures provided for different treatment of girls and boys. In 1951, the New York State legislature directed that girls ages 16 to 21 be subject to strict supervision and institutional commitment if they deserted their homes or deported themselves so as to endanger their morals or health.[7]

There was no comparable legislation directed to control male youths. Until declared unconstitutional in the late 1970s, legislation granted jurisdiction to the Juvenile Court over girls in need of supervision until they reached 18, but limited such jurisdiction over boys until they reached 16 years of age.

Under New Deal legislation, aid to dependent children had been based on loss of support from the father.[8] At 1961 hearings, "breadwinner" and "wage earner" were applied interchangeably to the father, and social benefits were conditioned on the unemployment of the father. Until challenged in the courts, no Federal matching, even for medical benefits, was allowed by reason of a mother's unemployment.[9] The Solicitor General argued that the difference in treatment of mothers and fathers was "gender-based" but "not gender-biased." However, the ACLU brief presented facts to counter this stereotyped presentation of the father as the wage-earner: in 1975 women were contributing 26% of family incomes; and 12% of the wives were contributing 50% or more of the family incomes.

Discrimination Against Unmarried Mothers and Their Children

Unmarried mothers and their children have been the objects of special harassment and discrimination by both states and the Federal government. After Alabama denied AFDC assistance to children whose mother was found to cohabit with an able-bodied man inside or outside the home, the issue was taken to the Federal Courts. The Supreme Court in 1968, with Earl Warren as Chief Justice, affirmed the holding of the lower Federal Court, that the Alabama law was inconsistent with the Social Security Act and with the Equal Protection Clause of the Constitution.[10] Known as the *King* decision, it held that, while states were not required to participate in the Federal program of AFDC, they could not benefit from its funding and also deny aid to a needy child because of a mother's behavior. The Supreme Court further noted that the suitable-home tests for deciding on aid to children had been "habitually used to disguise systematic racial discrimination." In a blunt concurring opinion, Justice Douglas wrote, "I would say that the immorality of the mother has no rational connection with the needs of her children under our welfare programs."

Louisiana had removed 23,000 children from the AFDC rolls under legislation disqualifying them from aid if an illegitimate child was born to a mother after she received public aid. On appeal by the Child Welfare

League of America and other social organizations, HEW Secretary Flemming ruled that "a state plan [AFDC] ... may not impose an eligibility condition that would deny assistance with respect to a needy child on the basis that the home conditions in which the child lives are unsuitable, while the child continues to reside in the home."

The 1968 *King* decision followed Secretary Flemming's path-breaking 1960 ruling.[11] At about the same time, Congress provided that dependent children could receive AFDC when placed in foster home care after a court determination that the family home was unsuitable. States required to choose between receiving Federal support for children in "unsuitable homes," or meeting the higher cost of foster home care themselves generally chose the former.

Added Harassment of Unmarried Mothers on Welfare

Ten years after the 1968 Supreme Court decision in *King*, some states engaged in new harassment of welfare mothers. In Alaska, an unmarried mother was required to answer a detailed questionnaire about her sexual activities with the putative father and other persons during the 10 months prior to the birth of her child and about her present relationship with any man. The use of such questions was defended on the ground that the Federal Administration in 1978 required them as a condition to the state receiving reimbursement. Federal audits went to great lengths to discover any overpayment by the states to mothers dependent on AFDC. In accord with the tradition of harassment, the Federal audit went so far as to question an allowance in New York for baby diapers beyond one year.[12]

In California, 500 raids on mothers receiving public assistance were conducted on one night. A social worker who refused to participate was fined for insubordination.[13] Mothers dependent on welfare were especially subject to charges of child neglect or mismanagement of funds. In Richmond, Virginia, 23 mothers who had borne more than one child out of wedlock were sent by welfare to a court for determination as to whether they were suitable mothers. In Florida, at one time, 45% of the mothers of children born out of wedlock withdrew applications for aid, fearing that their children would be taken away. Repeatedly, the marital status of a mother, rather than the needs or welfare of her child, determined state actions.

From Inattention to More Punishment

Discrimination against girls and women by legislation and in the courts reflected the traditional lesser interest in females. The famous 1967 "Report of the President's Commission on Law Enforcement and the Administration of Justice" failed to make any reference to female offenders in its 222 pages. The National Institute of Mental Health only recently made grants to "identify factors which appear to account for delinquency regardless of sex, and those factors which are sex specific." This belated interest occurred together with reports of a sharp rise in delinquency and crime among females. Arrests charging women with serious crimes increased by 52% between 1968 and 1973. More women were being convicted of crimes, and more were being sentenced to prison.

The Working Mother and Attacks on the Single Parent

Dated and unrealistic expectations for girls would only be of historical interest if they had not continued in new ways, despite vast changes in social mores and economic realities.

The steady increase in working mothers, their new aspirations, and the necessity for self-support do not fit neatly into the traditional patterns set by private charity or public welfare. By 1975 over 7 million families (one in eight) were headed by a single parent, generally the mother. Twenty-eight million children lived with working mothers. One out of three families headed by a single parent lived below the poverty line.

Conflicts about mothers who work have not been limited to the American political arena. In 1951, a committee of experts of the World Health Organization concluded that the use of day nurseries by working mothers caused "permanent damage to the emotional health of future generations." This conclusion was challenged as "without substantiating evidence and wrong" by Dr. Michael Rutter, a leading child psychiatrist in England. He wrote in 1976 of the harm resulting from knowing so many things that are not true. He also noted that "assertions of this kind have mostly been made by men."[14] The former president of the Carnegie Foundation wrote realistically, "Women must work, they want to work, and their labor is needed."[15]

The many laws and regulations intended to control misconduct by girls and women or reduce welfare costs were at odds with the failure to confront their responsibilities in today's world. The United States, unlike other industrialized countries in the western world, failed to come to grips with the needs of working mothers or those of their children. Small reforms were initiated, while the number of working mothers and the number of single parents grew by leaps. Research reports told that the largest increase among the mentally depressed is to be found among poor women who are single parents and among young married women working in low-paying jobs. The Federal answer since 1981 has been only to reduce aid for mothers and children and to eliminate job training and work opportunities for women.

In the late 1960s and early 1970s, the urge to put the genie of sex back in the bottle was weakened by changing mores, and intensified by fears among middle-class parents. In chambers, judges who had enforced traditional punishments for girls who violated the rules spoke of fears for their adolescent daughters. They told of daughters who were experimenting with sex and drugs, or who had left home. They were saddened by the widening alienation between their daughters and themselves. Yet, on the bench, these same judges often reverted to unyielding judgments on girls brought before them for similar misconduct. It was as though imposition of morality on other people's daughters would somehow restore the old order for their grandchildren, if not for their children.

In the words of one commentator, "Probably no part of our society has been so exclusively a male domain as the criminal justice system."[16] This was equally true of the Juvenile Justice system. It had been enacted, policed, and administered largely by men.

Chapter 8
The Ups and Downs of Mental Health in Juvenile Justice: A Tale of Shunning, Bundling, Denigration, and Survival

To a large extent, law and psychiatry have talked past each other despite the growth of sophistication in both disciplines.[1]

The coming of mental health services provided both high hope and some anxiety in the Juvenile Court. There was hope for medical treatment of mental retardation and mental illness. But there was also anxiety. The use of psychiatry to diagnose children was regarded both as a badge of honor that distinguished the Juvenile Court from other courts and as a reason for not regarding it as a real court.

In the early days of the Juvenile Court, an age for ardent amateurs, no special training was required for child-care workers, probation officers, or judges. The innocence of this period diminished as other professions showed greater interest in differences between children. When judges tried to respond, they found themselves thrust into a bramble patch that bristled with conflicting theories on the causes of mental, emotional, and behavioral problems and appropriate treatment.

Juvenile Courts were expected to resolve the problems of children that parents and the community were unable to handle. Small wonder that judges eagerly reached out to what were called "objective standards for certain answers." The first of such standards were provided by the Juvenile Court Clinic, established in 1917. At first it was given the narrow responsibility for providing findings on which mental defectives could be identified and institutionalized.

However, by the 1930s, the Clinic had come to do far more than separate "abnormal" from "normal" children. It had become a refuge for judges and probation officers when they did not know what to do with children or parents who seemed mentally disabled or seriously disturbed.

Greater acceptance of the Court Clinic was largely due to the rare qualities of its first director, Helen Montague, MD. With earthiness, patience, and good humor, she taught all who came her way, without intimating they needed to learn. She always seemed to sense how much knowledge judges or probation officers could tolerate. She smiled as she touched lightly on sexual problems and avoided issues that might prevent appropriate help for children. She had discovered ways to modify what Camus later called "the shopkeeper's morality."[2] Everyone, or almost everyone, in the Court, leaned on and turned to Dr. Montague for help in difficult cases.

One day, when a sullen adolescent in jeans (before they were common) was charged by her angry mother with refusal to attend school and with sleeping on rooftops, I sent them both to the Clinic. A short while later I noticed Dr. Montague, standing quietly in the rear of the courtroom, so I recessed court and asked her to come into chambers. She told me that the child had both male and female sexual organs, and lived in terror of discovery at school or by her sisters and brothers. She said her mother was ashamed of her. Baffled, we called my friend Viola W. Bernard, MD, who suggested an endocrinologist who had worked in this field. The endocrinologist offered to see the mother and child at once and admitted the child to his hospital service. She received psychiatric help to decide on a choice of sex. She decided that she wanted to be a girl and, after an operation, this child completed her education and later became highly successful in her chosen career. Such a miracle was rare and so was the chain of people who had brought it about.

The staff of the Clinic was never able to handle the growing referrals as more judges turned to it for advice. When diagnostics were secured, one could not secure the treatment services recommended by the Clinic. Probation officers needed help to select which children should be referred to the Clinic. One eminent psychiatrist, Marion E. Kenworthy, MD volunteered to meet with probation officers and social guidance staff, and she encouraged them to feel that they could make a difference in the lives of children. They met with her eagerly in those days after court hours.

In the mid-1930s, finding few treatment services for the children as recommended by the Clinic, I went to Boston hoping to find a model Juvenile Court. The Boston Court had an honorable tradition. The Judge Baker Guidance Clinic and famous researchers at Harvard were close geographically. But I found only rivalry: Drs. Sheldon and Eleanor Glueck spoke disparagingly of the Clinic as headed by an ex-gynecologist; the Clinic head described the Gluecks as compulsive book writers; and the Juvenile Court judge spoke contemptuously of both Harvard research and the Clinic, saying that he sent children to the Clinic only when they were "hopeless." The New York Court would have to make its own trails, despite the widespread fear of psychiatry and the lack of treatment services. Although psychoanalysis had become fashionable by the 1930s in well-to-do circles, it was regarded as unnecessary and unsuitable, if not dangerous, medicine for the poor.

The development of mental health services in the Juvenile Court moved forward in the face of agonizing obstructions. The Court, like schools and other agencies, seized upon the false promises of two pychologists who had promoted IQ tests as the best hope for achieving objective standards.

Goddard and Terman asserted in the 1920s that inborn intelligence could be measured, that in 80% of all cases it was determined by genetic factors, and that it could not be altered.[3] The early challenge by Allison Davis, that the focus should rather be on better schooling for potentially capable children, went unheeded.[4] It was not until the 1970s that Professor Leon Kamin of Princeton exposed the secret motivation of Goddard and Terman. They were determined to save Anglo-Saxon Americans from contamination by "inferior" breeds coming from South Eastern Europe and the Black Sea, and from the "taint of Negro blood."[5]

For decades, IQ findings were ground out for the Juvenile Courts. They were applied wholesale in schools through group tests and individually by clinics, including those that served the Juvenile Courts. These numerical findings, interpreted crudely if at all, were rarely questioned, although they determined the educational tracks to which children would be assigned.

Dependent on acceptance by voluntary agencies of children referred for residential care, the courts were locked into the arbitrary IQ conditions for admission. Some required a minimum of 80, others 85 or 90. As late as 1971, some state hospitals rejected mentally disabled adolescents if their IQs were not over 75.[6]

A probation officer was outspokenly critical of my efforts to find better schooling and treatment for a child who had suffered serious emotional damage from her parents because she only registered an 80 IQ. Years later, after special schooling and psychiatric treatment, this girl's achievements in college and a professional career showed how uncertain the certain test results had been.

Reliance for diagnosis on IQ tests alone also obscured what mental health services could do for underprivileged children. There were only a few psychiatrists who chose to work in areas where poverty and school failures were rampant. These were pioneers in social or community psychiatry.[7] An early study of three schools in Harlem, which contained a disproportionately high number of delinquent children, led to some hard questions that have still not been answered: Why did intelligence ratings and educational achievements begin to drop in the third grade and then continue to drop in these and other schools? What educational, emotional, and social factors were impairing the development of these children? The study touched on many sensitive spots in the school system, including the use of corporal punishment, inappropriate curriculum content, school suspensions, and racially discriminatory practices. Despite its distinguished sponsorship, the report's publication was delayed by the Board of Education, and ultimately distributed in only a limited edition after a 2-year period of stalling.[8]

With the approach and the arrival of World War II, mental health services for noncombatants was cut to pieces. It became all but impossible to secure treatment services even for children in desperate need.

It was not only the quantity but the quality of mental health services that suffered a serious decline. With its loss of staff and reduced budget, the Court Clinic was forced to hire staff on a part-time, hourly basis (9 to 29 hours a week). This part-time staff, with little time for children or parents and not knowing the facilities available, made recommendations with little regard for how or whether they could be implemented.

Conveyor-belt reports reflected the distancing of the part-time clinicians from the children. One psychiatrist predicted that because a 13-year-old boy got satisfaction and success from petty thefts, "more moral offenses would creep in, as his body matured." This physician told the mother in court that she was at fault, because she had had a child born out of wedlock, and that the boy should be put away. That night, the boy packed his clothes and left home. Before he was found, his mother returned to court.

In a low, but firm voice she said, "He is a child worth saving. I feel he would have behaved if he hadn't heard the doctor talk the way he did." She was right. When the boy was found and placed in more understanding hands, he did do well.

Another clinician predicted damnation for a 12-year-old Puerto Rican girl who had been victimized by dope peddlers when she first came to New York. He pronounced that although she was not "intrinsically vicious, her memories would linger so that her personality must be regarded as permanently warped." Still a third clinician protected all his bases, writing— of a boy charged with robbery—that "if he is a member of a gang, then he is a hoodlum. If he stays by himself then he is a schizoid." The diagnosis of schizoid was tossed about in those days as new wisdom, without anticipation that some years later thoughtful child and adolescent psychiatrists would condemn it as a "garbage-pail diagnosis."

For an adolescent who had shot his sister in a fit of anger, a caseworker set three high-sounding goals: to help the boy experience anxiety, to modify the rigidity of his personality, and to lift the repression of his guilt feelings and neurosis. These words did not fit a child who felt unloved, had been terrorized by a violent father, constantly dreamt of death, and had twice attempted suicide. Questioned about the need for more intensive therapy, the worker agreed it might be advisable, but stated the agency could not afford to provide psychiatric treatment for court children.

Overburdened staff in schools and in courts, unable to get psychiatric help for children, grew careless of dangers resulting from inaction. When Carmello was brought to court for shoplifting, probation discovered that he was on suspension from school for having tried to strangle two children 6 months earlier. The school explained that the strangling incident had occurred 2 months before the end of the school year when clinical studies were not available. In the fall he was left on suspension, but nothing had been done to get help for him or to protect other children.

One evening my husband urged me to speak to Dr. Kenworthy of my despair about getting treatment for children no matter what their needs. She suggested that short-term treatment services within the Clinic could offer one possibility. Presiding Justice John Warren Hill and Dr. Montague welcomed the plan, and Dr. Kenworthy agreed to develop a student fieldwork unit of the Columbia University School of Social Work in the Juvenile Court, and to raise funds for the program.[9] Some psychiatrists feared that involuntary treatment under court auspices could not be effective. This fear proved unfounded. In fact, Dr. Montague found that "moderately authoritarian" court referrals led to more regular keeping of appointments by the children and parents before they developed real relationships with their therapists.

Although the Treatment Clinic accepted difficult children in urgent need of help, 439 of 626 children (70% of the children) remained in their homes during its 8-year existence. Yet, despite the results, unanimous support from the judges and a positive evaluation of the Treatment Clinic by the New York Academy of Medicine, the City refused support. One more valuable mental health "demonstration" ended in 1945.

With the demise of the Treatment Clinic in 1945, judges could find no alternative mental health services. Bellevue Hospital and the Bureau of Child Guidance of the New York City Board of Education were overwhelmed. Parents were advised by schools and social workers to file delinquency petitions against their children as the only way to secure a psychometric test or diagnostic study. The Diagnostic Clinic at the Court was swamped, and the Court Administrator ordered that the Clinic limit its work to children and no longer see family members.

With 10,000 children brought before the Court in 1945, an increase of 57% over 1941, the Court still had only three part-time psychiatrists, the same as in 1917. Referrals by the Court for diagnostic studies had increased from 600 a year in 1925 to 1,611 in 1945. There were practically no openings for children in free or low-cost community clinics.

Juvenile Court judges were constantly faced with only two possible dispositions for mentally disabled, delinquent children. They could return them home, no matter how serious the risk to the family, the community and themselves, or they could commit them to a State Training School where no treatment services were available. New York State employed only one psychiatrist for hundreds of boys and none for the girls committed to its training schools in the late 1940s.

At war's end, a renewal of interest in mental health was kindled at the national and local levels of government. In 1952, the New York Juvenile Court made a first brave effort to obtain a profile of all children and parents referred to the Clinic by judges over a period of time. Molly Harrower, PhD, the psychologist for the Court Intake Project, reported that of 225 children referred:

76% were retarded in reading 2 or more years;
55% were retarded in reading 5 or more years;
80% came from low socioeconomic groups;
10% of the neglected children lived in families with a past history of
psychosis, or with marked psychotic trends in one parent currently.

This study made three noteworthy observations: (a) the psychological
tests used were not relevant to the population, and there was a need to devise
new tests; (b) the children showed little ability to express emotions and had
low expectations of what they could expect from their families or the outside world; and (c) although there were very few psychotic children in the
sample, a disproportionately large number of the parents were psychotic.[10]

From the vantage of his military leadership in wartime, William Men-
ninger, MD presented the needs of men and women rejected by the armed
services because of mental disabilities and of those who had suffered mental disabilities while in the service. He also spoke bluntly to members of the
psychiatric profession of having been appalled "to find how weak was the
voice and how vacillating the action of this loosely organized group [the
American Psychiatric Association, or APA] during the time of war. "[11] In
1946, a small group of distinguished psychiatrists responded and created
the Group for the Advancement of Psychiatry (GAP). Committed to multi-
professional study and to applying psychiatric data to the promotion of mental health, GAP did succeed in reforming and galvanizing the APA. Thus,
successive reports by GAP and APA study groups came to enrich and supplement each other. The APA, no longer a sleeping giant, became actively
concerned with relationships between psychiatry and social problems in this
country.[12,13]

The Federal response to the unmet needs for mental health services was
embodied in the National Mental Health Act (Public Law 487) of 1946, with
the establishment, in 1949, of the National Institute of Mental Health
(NIMH). Subsequently, Congress authorized other national efforts to assess
and improve mental health services, to identify unmet needs, and to make
recommendations for improvement, some of which were incorporated into
Federal legislation. [14,15,16]

Despite many delays in the development of services under these
Federal assessments, new gleams of hope appeared from Washington in the
early 1960s. President Kennedy confronted the neglect of the mentally disabled. A panel appointed by him defined mental retardation as a disabling

condition that should receive care. After Kennedy's assassination, President Johnson took up the cudgel and vigorously supported passage of the Mental Retardation Facilities and Community Mental Health Centers Construction Act of 1963 (Public Law 88-164), and the 1965 amendments to Title II of that Act (Public Law 89-105), which provided additional Federal funds for staffing community mental health centers.

In the spirit of the 1960s, Federal Courts began to examine the cruelty and neglect practiced against children in state institutions and to fashion remedies, including treatment plans for individual inmates. Some Federal Courts held for a short time that any person involuntarily institutionalized by reason of mental disability was entitled to treatment. This doctrine, setting forth the "right to treatment," was first enunciated by Justice David Bazelon, and was presented with careful guidelines: "A hospital need not show that the treatment will cure or improve him [the patient] but only that there is a *bona fide* effort to do so."[17]

In the leading case on the care of mentally disabled patients in the State Hospital of Alabama,[18] Chief Judge Franklin Johnson held in 1971 that "the purpose of involuntary hospitalization for treatment purposes is treatment and not punishment, and that the failure to provide treatment could not be justified by lack of funds."[19] In another class action, alleging many abuses in the Texas Training Schools, Judge William Wayne Justice ruled that juveniles had the constitutional right to adequate treatment plans and care that conformed to minimal professional standards.[20] Although later reversed on a procedural question, the decision achieved improvements for many delinquent youths in Texas. The Superintendent resigned, two of the worst facilities were closed, and Texas embarked on the development of community facilities for delinquents. Both decisions encouraged trial judges in the Juvenile Courts to accept more responsibility—at least for a time—for what happened to youth following dispositional orders.

However, judicial efforts to secure appropriate treatment for the mentally disabled were short-lived. They were undercut by disillusionment about the benefits of government intervention, skepticism about the value of psychiatric treatment, and by a drive to reduce mounting costs. In 1975, the Supreme Court held unanimously in *O'Connor v. Donaldson* that there was no constitutional basis for involuntary confinement of a person "dangerous to no one" who could live safely in freedom with the help of family or friends.[21] But, in his concurring opinion, Chief Justice Burger went further and expressed disagreement with the theory that the right to treatment was a quid pro quo for the loss of liberty. "Dangerousness," not the need for treatment, became the touchstone needed to justify hospitalization and involuntary treatment.[22,23]

With wishful thinking, the Appellate Court in the District of Columbia wrote that the Juvenile Court should use its expertise, secure in the knowledge that it is amply authorized to fulfill the rehabilitation purpose of the Act. In contrast, 4 years later, the Supreme Court expressed realistic concern over the "community's unwillingness to provide people and facilities," and over the "scarcity of professional help that impaired the work of the Juvenile Court."[24]

Reacting to the abuse of overhospitalization, the District of Columbia Court ordered the release of 42% of the patients at St. Elizabeth's Hospital to less secure facilities and mandated a plan for the care of each patient within 45 days.[25]

While hospitalization was being restricted, the Joint Commission on Mental Health of Children reported a woeful lack of psychiatric services for children throughout the country.[26] It found that of 1.4 million children in serious need of psychiatric services only 473,300, or 33.8%, were receiving such services. It criticized the maldistribution of mental health services, the failure to coordinate delivery of services, and the dearth in quantity and quality of psychiatric services for children. Untreated children were described as "bounced around from training school to reformatory, to jails, and whipped through all kinds of understaffed agencies [to] end up being treated more poorly than caged animals...."

Deterioration of Mental Health Services in the Juvenile Court

Even as Congress and state legislatures showed more concern for mental health, services deteriorated in the Juvenile Court.[27,28,29] Children had to wait for long periods in shelters, detention, and in hospitals for diagnostic studies. By 1970, the New York Court Clinic was operating solely in two of its five counties: Kings and New York. There was only one location in New York County where parents with mental health problems could be seen. In 1971, a study based on records and site visits, reported few treatment services for court children and extensive racial discrimination on the part of the voluntary agencies.[30]

In the late 1960s and early 1970s, additional funding cuts were imposed by the New York State Department of Mental Hygiene. The budget for retarded and mentally ill children was reduced. The mental health services at the Training Schools had been reduced to a purchase of limited hours from full-time state psychiatrists on their days off. The Court Clinic was restricted to doing diagnostics of children only when placement was contemplated. Beginning with the end of the 1960s, the Juvenile Court, also, faced the problems of turnstile children prematurely discharged from state hospitals without provision for continuing treatment in the community.

The director of adolescent services at Bellevue Hospital reported serious gaps in services for children under 16 years of age, including lack of facilities for antisocial adolescents not overtly psychotic; 1 1/2-year waiting lists at state schools for the mentally retarded; no facilities for active homosexuals or drug abusers if not psychotic; and no residential services for adolescents discharged by state hospitals.[31]

Legal Limits on Involuntary Treatment

Public defenders became ardent advocates in the late 1960s against court orders for the hospitalization of youth. They opposed involuntary placements as "coercive." They showed little concern for the right to admission for treatment except when "dangerousness" to self or others was evident. Nor did they show comparable opposition to obstacles to the admission of children whose illness required hospital treatment, nor to their clinically premature discharge back to the community.

A new twist or issue was raised in the 1970s by attorneys, who contended that mentally ill patients, hospitalized involuntarily, should have the right to refuse treatment. They argued that physicians had no right to impose treatment, although they had the duty to provide it when patients requested it. One judge ruled that patients had the "right to be wrong" or unwise in refusing treatment, so long as they did not endanger themselves or others.[32] In the same opinion, the judge denied damages for involuntary psychiatric treatment, finding that the state hospital psychiatrists had proven good faith and that they could not be held accountable when a state failed to provide necessary resources.

There was no meeting of the minds between those intent on protecting the civil liberties of the mentally disabled and those concerned over the consequences of nontreatment for young schizophrenics, abusers of drugs or alcohol, youthful delinquents, or lonely drifters. The absence of follow-ups on what happened to those denied or refusing psychiatric treatment left the debate heated but without data on which sound judgments could be based.

The new Federalism with its block grants to states did not increase mental health services for children. In 1971, the General Accounting Office reported to Congress that hardly 1% of the $137 billion appropriated in block grants to the states had been used for any services to children. The constantly shifting program interests of the Federal government did not include mental health services for youth.[33] The center of interest moved to generalized preventive service, to runaways, to the separation of noncriminal (status) offenders from criminal offenders, and to fashioning "just deserts" for minors. By 1977 the National Institute for Mental Health did not even include any special requirements for the treatment of children as mandated by the Community Mental Health Centers Act.

The Drive for Deinstitutionalization

Rooted in revulsion against the endless holding of harmless inmates in the back wards of state hospitals, the drive for deinstitutionalization was also steamed by resentment over the rising costs of care. More concern was expressed for the overuse of hospitalization than for the wrongful denial of long-term residential treatment when indicated. In 1963, two eminent psychiatrists in New York found a crippling shortage of professional staff in public agencies and the creaming of patients by voluntary agencies to be contributing causes to both overtreatment and undertreatment. The poorest and most deprived children had been passed from one physician to another in clinics without full study.[34]

States increasingly restricted hospital care to children who were overtly psychotic. Hospitalization was denied when the treatment of choice by physicians was disregarded as the criterion for admission. State hospitals closed intake, accepting children only as others were released.[35] Children dangerous to themselves or others were left in the community or returned to the community prematurely without adequate aftercare. Voluntary agencies continued selective intake. Diagnostic studies declined, and waiting periods for care of mentally disabled children stretched out for months. In New York, a 1971 study revealed that, for 55% of the delinquents found mentally disabled and in need of treatment, no placement was available other than the Training School for delinquents.[36]

State rules requiring dangerousness for hospitalization and the drive for deinstitutionalization had serious repercussions on the work of the Juvenile Court. When I questioned why one youth, who had a history of four suicide attempts, was returned to court within 24 hours and without a full study, the psychiatrist from the city hospital replied that current policy did not allow involvement in past history in the absence of current dangerousness.[37] New York limited admission to patients who were "homicidal, suicidal, or dangerous," overruling recommendations of city hospitals that a child or youth who was mentally disturbed needed long-term treatment.

Pressures on the hospitals for discharge also invited abuse by staff eager to rid themselves of serious management problems. After escaping from a state hospital, 15-year-old John was found wandering on the streets of New York. Readmitted to the state hospital on recommendation of a city hospital, he was quickly discharged to his own custody. Again picked up by the police as he wandered aimlessly, he was sent to a different state hospital when the former hospital rejected him, with the excuse that his family had recently moved and that he therefore belonged in a different catchment area. The real reason for rejection was that his behavior had caused many problems.

State hospitals also rid themselves of neglected and abused children when they became difficult to control. Bernard, an abused child, was sent to a state hospital when his behavior became bizarre after experimenting with LSD. Discharged to abusive relatives, he set fires and scalded his grandmother with boiling water. After a second hospitalization he was again discharged to the same "family," only to be re-hospitalized when he assaulted other family members.

A further difficulty arose from the fact that State Hospitals had long functioned as though the problems of minors could be handled with fewer staff and at less cost than care for adults. In Massachusetts, minors comprised 40% of the state hospital population, but received only 20% of the budget. This was typical of budget allocations in many states.

Discharges of mentally disabled youths without plans for community support were doubly threatening when families could not or would not provide a home. Youths could not go to single-room occupancy hotels. They were not entitled to independent welfare support. They became flotsam passed between relatives, shelters, detention, and a variety of institutions, with none prepared or eager to accept them.

Opinions on the results of the drive for deinstitutionalization depend on which figures one chooses to read. In New York, there was pride that the median length of stay in state hospitals declined from the monstrous 217 days in 1958 to 38 days in 1973. Discharges of patients had increased from 9,554 in 1955 to 35,960 in 1973. Less happy figures showed that readmissions to state hospitals had soared from 27% in 1955 to nearly 65% in 1974, that state funds allocated for community treatment after discharge were woefully inadequate and bore no relation to the increase in discharges.

The Rights of Children Versus Parents

Court decisions on the rights of children reflected conflicting and changing views about the rights of parents. In *Parham*, the lower court held that parents and guardians could not waive the right of children under 18 to counsel and a hearing, prior to hospitalization for mental disability. Four years later, the Supreme Court castigated the lower court for an overdose of due process, and expressed the faith that parents would act in the best interest of their children. It criticized the lower court for directing the state of Georgia to provide noninstitutional resources for mentally disabled children as "substantive due process." A note of irritation, if not exasperation, crept into the majority opinion: "Ironically as most states have expanded these efforts to assist the mentally ill, their actions have been subjected to increasing attacks."[38,39]

However, Justice Brennan (in a separate opinion) wrote of the "thousands of elderly patients now confined to the back wards of ... state institutions, first admitted as children...." He also warned of possible conflicts between parents and children, and wrote that when a public agency acted in the role of guardian, the rights of children deserved special scrutiny. Finally, moving beyond the concept of equal rights for children, Justice Brennan wrote, "Indeed, it may well be argued that children are entitled to more protection than adults." No pursuit of this viewpoint is yet found in later decisions of the Supreme Court.

The 1970s, which had begun with a big legal bang for "the right to treatment" under law, went out with a whimper for children and youth in need of mental health services. Fiscal restraints and the limitations imposed by the Supreme Court on intervention in "state rights" had emasculated the right to treatment. By the 1980s the right to refuse treatment had been more firmly established than the right to receive treatment. Demands for community protection from troubling youth, together with drives for deinstitutionalization, brought more homeless disturbed youths to shelters, to the streets, and back to the Juvenile or Criminal Courts. More youths were left "untended and untreated."

Juvenile Justice Restricted by Institutional Racism

From the outset, when Goddard and Terman were bent on using IQ tests to protect this country from the "taint of Negro blood," the administration of Juvenile Justice has been confounded by many controls imposed by institutional racism.

Prior to the 1960s, mental health services were practically nonexistent for nonwhite children brought before the Juvenile Court. The comforting theory had been developed that a capacity for verbal communication was essential to psychotherapy. "Nonconceptual thinking" had become code words for not accepting nonwhite children by voluntary treatment services. These code words, although unspoken, had been translated into policies and practices by both government and voluntary agencies.

In New York two voluntary agencies, one Catholic and one Jewish, both predominantly used for white children, had acquired increased public funding for children in need of residential mental health care. It was only after the Protestant Federation protested that the City had made no provision for the large number of young black Protestant children that the Wiltwyck School was added as a third treatment agency. The Comptroller for the City introduced a resolution that Wiltwyck should receive the higher compensation allowed for mental health services for 50% of its population, so equaling the number of children for whom the higher payments were being paid to the Catholic and Jewish agencies. Judge Hubert Delany and I protested to the Board of Estimate that the City did not limit treatment of tuberculosis on a religious or racial basis. The Bronx Borough President rose and expressed admiration that a Jew*esssss* "should plead the cause of Negro children." The *S*s were interminable, but the resolution was amended to authorize treatment for all the children at Wiltwyck.

Racial discrimination added to the injuries to nonwhite youth in need of mental health service throughout the country. The Childrens' Defense Fund found that white children under 14 were twice as likely to have had outpatient treatment prior to admission to state hospitals than nonwhites, and that nonwhite children were more likely to be discharged without referral for outpatient aftercare.[40]

The Abuse of IQs for Black Children

In the late 1930s and 1940s, black children were classified in large numbers as dull-normal or retarded, with IQs generally reported to range between the low 60s and high 70s. Voluntary agencies and state schools rejected them as unsuitable for their programs. Based on the IQ reports—mostly mass administered and culturally inappropriate—children were often excluded without being seen. Even some Court clinicians seemed to look at test scores more avidly than at the children. Hattie, a shy 12-year-old, was brought to court for truancy. Both parents worked at unskilled, changing jobs. Hattie stayed home and cleaned the house for a large family. She preferred this to school where she was far behind other children of her age. She caused no trouble and her mother spoke of Hattie as a great help. Still, the clinician who saw her was only troubled that her performance IQ (87) was 17 points higher than her verbal IQ (70).

Significantly, as the years passed, the IQs reported on black children by schools and clinics inched upward. Tests that had clustered black children below 80 moved into the 80 to 90 range, with more reports of higher IQs. In 1944-1945, when I examined the records of all the children brought to the New York County Juvenile Court during several months, the IQ reports showed no disparity between white and black children. Of 139 children found in need of placement by the Court, 66 were white and 73 were black. Four white children had IQs under 70; there were no black children with such low scores. There were 38 white and 46 black children with reported scores between 70 and 90. In the range of 90 or over, 24 were white and 27 were black.

No research offered an explanation for the aggregate rise in the IQs of black children. One could only wonder about possible causes, such as longer removal from the South, better nutrition and physical care, fuller adjustment to city life, increased education of parents, greater interest of black parents in the education of their children, changes in tests that made them less prejudicial to black children. For the most part, the old tests (with exceptions) had failed to consider language barriers; cultural differences; deterrants to verbal skills; or economic, social, and emotional problems that lowered performance results.

It was not until 1967 that a Federal Court held that IQ testing, based on an English-speaking population, used for school assignments of poor black children in the nation's capital, violated their right to equal opportunity.[41] Twelve years later another Federal Court ruled that the racially and culturally biased IQ tests used in California had resulted in a disproportionate number of black children placed in classes for the mentally retarded.[42]

The 1980s: Distancing and Denial of Mental Health Services

Beginning in the mid-1970s, the Supreme Court moved steadily away from the acceptance of Federal responsibility for overseeing or improving state action in regard to the welfare and mental health of children as well as of adults. In 1977, it had held that the 8th Amendment protection against cruel and unusual punishment did not prohibit corporal punishment of public school children.[43] It criticized lower Federal Courts that concerned themselves with substantive rights rather than limiting the issues before them to procedural due process. By the mid-1980s, the Supreme Court invoked the doctrine of "state sovereignty" to overrule a lower court that directed Pennsylvania to correct violations of its own laws regarding conditions in state hospitals.[44] In his dissent to this 5-4 decision, Justice Stevens called it "a voyage into the sea of undisciplined law-making."

The Federal administration also reduced aid to the mentally disabled. It abruptly terminated Social Security payments to thousands of the disabled. This assault on the mentally ill was characterized by Justice Jack Weinstein (Chief Judge, U.S. District Court of New York) as "evidence of the fixed clandestine policy against those with mental illness."[45,46] Only this decision, other Federal Court decisions, and the threat of Congressional action forced the Federal administration to modify its arbitrary actions to reduce aid to the mentally disabled in laggard fashion.

One evening, I met again with a distinguished Federal judge, Morris Lasker, who had issued path-breaking decisions in the 1970s to correct health, mental health, educational, and recreational deprivations imposed on children held in public institutions. As we talked, I asked whether he thought such decisions would be upheld on appeal by the present Supreme Court. He smiled enigmatically and answered, "I do not know."

One Small Effort of Long Ago

Late that same evening, I recalled a slender volume given to me by Marion Kenworthy years earlier. It contained the first 12 annual reports, beginning in 1904, of the Garden State Colony for the chronically insane in Massachusetts. She had started her professional life there as the first "woman assistant physician."

The Colony had been placed on a remote farmland tract for the purpose of helping mentally ill patients become self-supporting. At first, men had been taught to log, cart timber, and farm, whereas women were allowed only to pick berries on supervised walks. Later, the work of women included mending clothes for all the inmates, rug weaving, and mending household linens. Early annual reports spoke of the increasing mental activity and morale of patients as they learned to work. Later reports told of the lesser need for physical restraints when patients lived in smaller living units that respected privacy and when men and women were placed in adjacent buildings with a communal dining room. A library and patient orchestra were added. One superintendent wrote of the importance of not treating the mentally ill like kindergarteners or assuming acute illness when that phase had passed. As patients were found to improve, staff looked for boarding homes when no family members could be found to accept the patients, and these boarding homes were visited by the physicians each Sunday.

In the 1914 report, the superintendent wrote that the Colony had normalized life and increased the efficiency of patients, but concluded, "We have done very little to brighten their lives." Yet, this small effort, like many others, motivated some physicians to do more for mentally ill patients. Their work stood in sharp contrast to the later equation of freedom with nonhelp to the mentally disabled.

As more mentally disabled youth passed through Juvenile Courts, mental health services had been rendered practically nonexistent. The revolving door had replaced the back ward. The National Institute of Mental

Health announced in 1981 that it would no longer fund direct services and would provide only technical assistance in the future.[47]

Contradictory Demands on Psychiatry

As throughout the history of psychiatry, contradictory demands were made on it in the 1980s. The attempted assassination of President Reagan brought new attacks on the insanity defense and against psychiatrists who testified as expert witnesses for defendants. At the same time, psychiatrists were called on to predict which offenders should be treated as "dangerous" for the purpose of longer confinement to protect the community.

Psychiatrists responded to expectations for prediction in widely different ways. Some were willing to be called as expert witnesses to identify dangerous offenders. Others wanted no part in such a role. The American Psychiatric Association took the position that psychiatrists should not be expected to predict future violence or to render judgments on the sanity of offenders, and should do no more than testify on their medical findings.

There was controversy between psychiatrists about procedures for the release of the mentally disabled from hospitals. Psychiatrists recognized the good intention and the benefits that had resulted from freeing patients from overly long detention in state hospitals. They also contended that the freedom gained was not enough for large numbers of patients suffering from serious or chronic mental illness. Law and psychiatry were still talking past each other.

At a different level, psychiatrists in social and community psychiatry emphasized the sociocultural and economic conditions that they saw as contributing to the inadequate functioning, aggressive behavior, and emotional maladjustments of children, youths, and adults trapped in poverty. They looked more closely at individual children and groups of youths who suffered from social neglect. Long a small group, these psychiatrists grew in influence as they bridged the gap between knowledge of mental health and illness and the limited application of such knowledge to the mentally disabled.

Psychiatric guidance was sought by lawyers and judges when involved in court battles between parents over custody and support. However, it was rarely used when there were no parents to battle for the custody of a child.

Although psychiatry was used in many different ways, criticism of the "medical model" continued, as though there were only one model.

Beyond the conflicting viewpoints concerning psychiatry and the uses of mental health knowledge, two vast shadows continue to dominate the scene. The growing numbers of mentally disabled and the cost for their care has risen year after year. Even those least concerned with the human costs could not ignore the report from the National Institute of Mental Health that nearly one out of five adults (18.7%) suffers mental illness during their lives.[48]

In 1984, the American Psychiatric Association presented the tragedies resulting from dumping chronically mentally ill patients back into communities to wander about, uncared for and homeless.[49] It challenged the Reagan myth of "homeless by choice." This report recalled the still-unfulfilled goals for mental health set forth by Dr. Isaac Ray 150 years ago:

- Concern for the rights as well as the medical needs of the mentally ill;
- Just laws for commitment and the moral right to treatment;
- Concern for the relationship between insanity and social issues such as the proper care and the rights of the indigent.

Chapter 9
Religious Separatism

The First Amendment, with its inseparable prohibitions against restricting the free exercise of religion and against providing support for religion, was the answer of the founding fathers to religious bigotry in early America. In *The Liberties of an American*, Leo Pfeffer described how those bigotries had affected religious minorities:

> At the outbreak of the Revolutionary War, it was illegal to celebrate mass in any of the colonies other than Pennsylvania. In two-thirds of the colonies, a particular church was established as the official state religion, toward the support of which all were obliged to contribute. In Virginia, a Christian who denied the Trinity was punishable with imprisonment for three years and could be adjudged an unfit custodian of his children. Baptists were frequently whipped, beaten, arrested, fined and imprisoned, sometimes on bread and water.[1]

Fruits of the First Amendment were described by James Bryce years after its adoption: "All religious bodies are absolutely equal before the law, and unrecognized by the law, except as voluntary associations of private citizens." To this he attributed the absence of strife from different theological claims that had prevailed in other countries.[2] But by the 20th century, commitment to the separation of church and state had become less inviolable as religious institutions grew in strength and asserted political power.

Demand for Religious Conformity

Religious separatism held special consequences for children in the Juvenile Court. Repeatedly, those adults assigned to protect religious integrity often became zealots. This had been true before the days of the First

Amendment. In early America, children were subjected to four masters: parents, persons to whom they were apprenticed, the church, and the state. Throughout American history charitable giving had been treated as largely exempt from laws and decisions requiring separation of church and state. Voluntary associations felt free to act as though they were not bound by the First Amendment.

By the 1930s, some agency representatives and public officials in New York acted like policemen on behalf of sectarian agencies. They were quick to report any nonconformist behavior of children, parents, and even judges. Eavesdropping made judges hesitant to discuss religious issues with one another. Pressure for religious conformity affected what they said and did in and outside the courtroom. Many felt it politically expedient to participate in religious ceremonies of all faiths on ceremonial occasions.

On the Eastern seaboard, Jews and Catholics, fearful of Protestant proselytizing, had organized federations to strengthen their faiths and to raise funds for sectarian services. Each developed a vigorous life of its own with political clout. The major sectarian groups established the doctrine that religious teaching under one roof was essential to adult religious adherence. None extended this concern to nonwhite children, and all engaged in racial discrimination.

It was not until 1946, that the administrative code in New York was amended to prohibit public funding to any charitable agency that denied admission to children, duly committed by the Commissioner of Welfare or the Juvenile Court, because of race, color, or religion. However, this first local prohibition contained a large religious escape clause. It provided that "no institution of a particular religious faith shall be required to accept children adhering to a religious faith other than its own."[3] This exception did not satisfy a number of agencies that withdrew from accepting children from the city. They accepted only white children of their faith until rising costs and decreased private placements forced them to again accept children from the city.

The New York Juvenile Court of the 20th century did not reflect either the bigotry of the pre-First Amendment period or the atmosphere free of religious strife described by Bryce. It imposed practices rooted in sectarian volunteerism. Almost everyone and most institutions were identified as Protestant, Catholic, or Jewish. But, when one Juvenile Court judge asserted at a judicial meeting that no judge who did not accept the divinity of Christ was fit to sit on the case of a Catholic child, this went too far, and his colleagues of all faiths expressed disagreement.

Separatism Enforced by the Court

In 1935, among the first legal documents presented to guide a judge was one from the New York City Department of Welfare. It stated that the State Charities Law required placement of children "under the control of persons of the same religious faith when practicable." It asserted any deviation was to be explained by the judge in the minutes of the court hearing.

The New York Constitutional Convention in 1938 limited financial support for children placed in state institutions or institutions controlled by persons of their faith when practicable. This provision reaffirmed the religious separation that had long been practiced by child welfare and the Juvenile Court. Judges regularly imposed religious obligations on children and parents; civil servants were appointed and assigned as probation officers to families on the basis of religion; and the placement of children by religion had become routine practice with little regard for the best interest of individual children.

Adoptive parents were required to promise that they would bring up a child within a specific religion. If the husband and wife were of different faiths they had little chance of adopting a child. Agnostics, atheists, members of the Ethical Culture Society, and other humanists were rejected out of hand.[4]

A far different viewpoint was expressed by a member of the Catholic clergy in 1957. At a conference in Pennsylvania, Father Snee spoke strongly in support of the First Amendment and for freedom of religion:

> Any discussion of religion in adoption and custody cases should be governed by a consideration of four principles: the principle of disestablishment provided by the First Amendment, by which all religions have equal status before the law; the principle of freedom of religion, which includes also the freedom to choose no religion; the right of parents or those who hold the place of parents to educate their children; and the principle that the welfare of the child has priority over other considerations.[5]

Such adherence to the First Amendment, concern for religious freedom, and the well-being of children had been outlawed in New York as antireligious by sectarian agencies, by the laws of the state, and by court decisions.

Nonsectarianism Undermined

The vision and practice of nonsectarian giving on the basis of need, rather than on religious adherence, dwindled in the 20th century. Nonsectarian agencies had shown concern for children of all faiths, although they had not confronted racial discrimination. Standing proud in their beliefs, these nonsectarian agencies were shoved aside into a second-class category by public officials under sectarian pressure. They were used only for the allocation of Protestant children or those rejected by all agencies of a child's faith. This was the policy of the Department of Welfare and the Juvenile Court in New York.

Anne's mother had chosen to place her daughter in a nonsectarian agency, and supported her while she worked. On losing her job, she sought aid from the Welfare Department to continue Anne where she had placed her, saying Anne was doing well and that she did not want her moved to a Catholic institution, although she was Catholic. When I approved the mother's plan, the Commissioner of the Department of Welfare wrote, "I wonder if it was your intention to direct the placement of this Catholic child to a nonsectarian agency without seeking a placement in an institution of the child's religious faith." No reference was made to what uprooting this adolescent would mean to the child, or to her mother. Next, I learned that the city official had cleared the case with Catholic Charities under an unwritten agreement to clear all placements "out of religion." The confidentiality of records was violated. When I failed to change my decision, the City held up reimbursement to the nonsectarian agency, not only for Anne but for all children in its care. After 4 months, the City reimbursed for the care of the other children, but refused to do so for Anne until Catholic Charities "approved" the placement. It was never clear whether the City's punitive action was intended to punish the mother, to warn me against such action in the future, or to deter nonsectarian agencies from accepting non-Protestant children.

In one published manual, the City announced that in referring children for placement, the wishes of the parents were "to be considered when they were *not* Catholic, Protestant or Jewish." This exception, allowing consideration of the wishes of only a few Greek Orthodox or Muslim parents, revealed how far the city accepted the position that the three established religions had a claim superior to that of parents in deciding on the welfare of their children.

In 1936, a first baptism by religious fire descended on my head when four neglected children were brought before me for placement. The mother, a Roman Catholic, had been married to the father, a Muslim, by a Protestant minister. During one of their many quarrels, the mother had the oldest boy baptized in the Catholic Church without the knowledge of the father. When a daughter was born, the father retaliated by having her initiated into Islam against the mother's wishes. Having thus punished each other, neither parent had done anything about the religion of the next two children. None of the four children had received any religious education. The case was brought by Catholic and Protestant institutions to whom the children had been allocated. Religious baptism became the central issue. The oldest boy, baptized in the Catholic faith, was now 15, swarthy and tall. He wanted to live with a caring paternal uncle and be a Muslim. The 13-year-old girl, who had been initiated in the Muslim faith, was blonde and blue-eyed like her mother. She feared her father and wished to be Catholic.

After a full investigation and a study of the law, I held that infant baptism did not make a child the property of any church, and placed the elder boy with his uncle and the girl with a Catholic agency, holding that "There are no interests entitled to consideration except those of the parents and the children."[6] The first public response was a scare headline in the Brooklyn *Tablet* (a sensationalist tabloid newspaper published by the Brooklyn Diocese): "Daughter of Rabbi Wise Gives Child of Christ to the Black Bearded Prophet of Mohammed." The placement of the daughter in a Catholic agency was not mentioned. Shortly after this article appeared, a friendly Catholic judge called at my home and said that the Cardinal was deeply troubled by my decision. I told him of the family history and how the parents had used religious baptism only to hurt one another. Asked what he would have done, he answered, "I don't know, but why did you have to write an opinion?" I explained that I could find no recent decisions in New York involving religious controversies between parents. It therefore seemed only right to give the reasons for my decision. Our discussion ended and we understood one another, although I knew he was disappointed not to have secured acceptance of infant baptisms as the determining factor in the placement of children.

Infant baptism continued to control the lives of many children. In 1950 two brothers, ages 6 and 2, were separated by another judge, although both had been baptized in the Greek Orthodox faith by their parents. When the mother died and the father sought placement, a baptismal certificate was produced showing that the older boy had been baptized in another faith in a city hospital. Although this baptism was without the knowledge or consent of either parent, the judge held that the child belonged to that faith and must be placed accordingly.

Role of State, City, and Voluntary Agencies in Religious Separatism

Both state and city officials averted their eyes from misplacements and the denial of quality services, as long as children were placed within religion. Judges and caseworkers became desensitized to the needs of individual children as they blindly accepted the law and practices of religious separatism.[7]

Although the New York State Department of Welfare was responsible for the care of all children placed outside their homes, it fudged when powerful religious bodies were involved. Although staff was required to visit all child-caring institutions, their reports reflected the political power of boards more accurately than the needs of children under care. Standards for numbers and qualifications of staff varied from institution to institution. For years, these reports were held secret except from the chairmen of agencies involved. Judges and local welfare officials were not allowed to see evaluations of agencies to which they were required to send children.

At times, city officials became the enforcers of religious separatism. When a Protestant child was left by her sick mother in the care of a Catholic friend, the City Welfare Department disapproved the home although the child was receiving excellent care. Refusing subsidy to the foster mother, the City Bureau Chief wrote to me: "Ordinarily in accordance with the New York State law and agency policy, we would refer the child to a Protestant agency. Since the request for aid involves approval for placement of a Protestant child in a Catholic home, we would be unable to be of service."[8] Only after months of my battling in the name of an independent judiciary did the Welfare Department agree to pay for foster home care in the home chosen by the mother.

Few judges or social agencies were willing to tilt with the vast welfare windmill that controlled the purse as well as lives of applicants for aid. When two healthy toddlers were held in congregate care and denied foster home care because they were nonwhite, the public agency and five other agencies (Protestant and nonsectarian) all refused to provide care. The explanation or excuse was that the children were Catholic and had been allocated to an agency of the Catholic faith by the Welfare Department.

Separation of Staff by Religion

Probation officers were long appointed on a dual quota basis—by religion and by color. Only a probation officer of the child's religion could be assigned to a case. Black probation officers could be assigned only black children, although white probation officers could be assigned to white or black families. In August 1941, the New York State legislature went further, requiring that, when there were children in a family, staff should also be assigned to the case on the basis of religion.[9]

Probation officers of the three faiths, with some noticeable exceptions, acted like members of exclusive clubs who talked and ate separately. They were instructed by supervisors and by some judges on their obligation to strengthen the religious affiliations of those entrusted to their care. Attending to religious obligations was made a condition of probation for a child by many judges. The religious devotion of parents and children was presented as a test of morality in the home. A few judges required children to recite the Ten Commandments in court and tailored their dispositions to the regularity of a child's religious observance.

The appointment and assignment of civil servants (probation officers) on the basis of religion was not challenged until the 1960s, when the American Jewish Congress brought an action against the Presiding Justice. Following that action, and a critical article by Harrison Salisbury in *The New York Times*, Dean James Pike of the Cathedral of St. John the Divine invited my husband and me to attend his service the following Sunday. We observed the impressive procession and listened to superb music. Then Dean Pike mounted the high pulpit in the great cathedral. He began his sermon by asking his parishioners to look about them and gaze at the beautiful stained glass windows. Then, the Dean thundered, "You see, if we had limited ourselves to Episcopalians, we could not have filled the windows."

He then attacked any religious test for government employment as a violation of the First Amendment.

Willful Cruelty

Willful cruelty, born of religious fanaticism, rarely appeared in the Juvenile Court. But a few decisions caused deep cleavages. One case remains unforgettable. In the spring of 1949, an elderly Jewish refugee from the holocaust brought two little girls, ages 5 and 6, to court as neglected children. Their mother had left them with her, but failed to make the promised board payments and had disappeared. The foster mother testified that the mother had told her that the children were Jewish, that their grandfather was a Rabbi in Brazil, and that she wanted her children raised in the Orthodox Jewish tradition. When the mother failed to appear in answer to court process, a finding of neglect was made without prejudice, and the children were committed to a Jewish agency for adoption.[10] On the mother's reappearance some months later, she demanded the return of her children, and claimed they were Catholic. After extensive hearings, the judge found that the mother had reappeared only when faced with the threat of deportation, and that the claim of baptism was only a "device trumped up for lack of a meritorious case." He also found the mother to be an unfit guardian and confirmed the previous finding of neglect.[11] After visiting the children in their adoptive home, the judge wrote "I cannot in good conscience deprive them now of what may well be their last chance of good lives and set them wandering on the *via dolorosa* of institutional or shifting foster home placement." On the religious issue Judge Sicher, a meticulous legal scholar, added, "The court will not itself prefer one church to another but will act without bias for the welfare of the child under the circumstances of each case."

On appeal, the Juvenile Court was reversed. The Appellate Court held that if the mother was an unfit guardian, the children should have been turned over to some Catholic agency.[12] Infant baptism without regard to the welfare of children was again treated as the sole criterion for placement. Despite briefs by the Louise Wise adoption agency, the Citizens' Committee for Children of New York, the Episcopal Diocese, and the Spence-Chapin Adoption Society urging that the children not be taken from their loving adoptive home, the Court of Appeals denied review. In the words of

Shad Polier, counsel for the adoption agency, the Children's Court had been transformed from guardian of children to an agent for religious groups.

On the appointed day, the two little girls, now 7 and 8, weeping hysterically, clung to their adoptive parents, and refused to recognize their mother. One cried out that she had never loved them. Yet, they were forced to go with the mother and a lawyer assigned by the Church. The lawyer had told the court the children would be placed in a good Catholic home, or with a "rehabilitated mother." Neither promise was kept.

Sixteen years later, the director of the adoption agency called me in great excitement. The one-time adoptive mother had just phoned and told her of a miracle. The adoptive mother had received a phone call in which a happy voice had said, "If you're not sitting down, you'd better do so. You're going to get a shock. This is Diane." Her story tumbled out. She had run away from the last placement, gone to Chicago, finished school, and was married. She and her young husband had come East to find her adoptive parents. Her only clue was a scrap of paper with the name of the town in which they had lived and the memory of their name. She had hidden it when the toys given to her by her adoptive parents had been taken away. Some days later Diane visited and told of many unhappy placements for her and her sister. They never lived with their mother. They had not forgiven their mother or the Church for taking them from the "only real mother and father" they had ever known.

Such cruel abuse of religion was unusual. More common injuries to children resulted from strict adherence to practices followed routinely in the name of religion. If no agency of a child's faith was available, a child might be forced to wait months and even years in temporary shelter, inappropriate institutional care, or be returned to an unfit home. The Juvenile Court and Department of Public Welfare were both party to such denials of appropriate care.

Parents were not told why their children waited for care in temporary shelters, nor that they had any choice in the referrals for placement. In 1951, the chief probation officer in the New York Juvenile Court issued a directive, "There shall be no indication by the probation officer to the parent or child of the specific institution to which the child is to be referred until such time as the judge has determined the institution and the institution has accepted the child."[13]

The Dominance, Ebb, and Return of Religious Separatism and Racial Segregation

When the witch hunts after World War I receded, a period of ecumenism dawned. More citizens sought understanding and appreciated differences. But, after World War II, demands for greater religious conformity grew again in the Juvenile Court, in schools, and in universities as in the political marketplace. Religious conformity was imposed as a litmus test of anticommunism. This period of oppression faded in the 1960s, when greater support for civil rights and dissent again encouraged ecumenism.

In the Juvenile Court, criticism grew against the exclusion of children from care by reason of religion or race. Secret quotas diminished in the 1970s. Public defenders had become active advocates in the court on behalf of the rights of children, regardless of race or religion.

This review of religious separatism and its effect on the lives of children from the 1930s to the 1970s might seem superfluous if this were not the late 1980s. Today, the Reagan administration and the radical right are joined in undermining the First Amendment and the decisions under which separation of church and state have protected freedom in America.

Seepage from attacks on the First Amendment are reaching local communities. In 1984, the City of New York required that all foster parents be identified and categorized by race and religion. The code word used to justify such markings was again called *matching*. Once more, poor parents and children, dependent on public welfare, were subjected to religious separatism and racial segregation in violation of the First and Fourteenth Amendments. In December 1986, a Federal Court decision, holding that children referred to tax-supported voluntary agencies should be accepted without discrimination based on religion or racial grounds, came under heavy attack. It was characterized by the representatives of two major sectarian federations as violating their "mission to care for children of their own religion."

Chapter 10
Racial Discrimination

Our courts do not bear the responsibility for initiating positive measures to correct the centuries-old abuses of the Negro.[1,2]

This reality presented the most painful and humbling of lessons to me as a judge of the Juvenile Court. Compliance with unjust treatment—imposed by law, tradition, and institutional practices—became a recurrent nightmare. It was lightened only by the rescue of a few children and by efforts (after court hours) to help change systems that treated black children as inferior. How to outrun, or to find ways around, traditional injustice became an urgent, if not conventional, judicial avocation.

The 1930s

In the 1930s, judges, like other citizens, were less self-conscious about their prejudices. At the first state meeting of judges that I attended, the chairman spoke of the difference between upstate delinquents and the metropolitan "devils." He urged that the latter be placed in separate state schools. When I questioned racial segregation, he replied in unctuous fashion that he respected and liked his "colored" servants. There could be little communication with those who saw segregation and inferior treatment of black children as natural and right.

At the first White House Conference for Children in 1907, Booker T. Washington had stated that there were practically no black children in southern orphan asylums, because "Negroes had been trained to know they must take care of their own." With prescience, he also expressed fear of what would happen if blacks moved to northern cities and lost responsibility for one another. Two years later, Mary Ovington, an outstanding social worker in New York, wrote that blacks could live only in the worst places and pay the highest rents, while their children were learning "the rude manners of the street." In the South, as in the North, there was little community concern for the well-being of the black child during the next half-century.

In 1935, the Juvenile Court, like schools, colleges, adult courts, and voluntary institutions, practiced racial discrimination with little self-questioning. Exclusion by voluntary agencies was taken for granted. Children's Village, a nationally respected institution for children, publicized its program as "a private, nonsectarian, cottage-type training school, equipped for the study, education and development of white problem boys and girls, surrendered by parents or committed by Children's Courts."[3]

Despite a doubling of the black population in New York City between 1920 and 1930, few services or facilities had been added for black children. The Commissioner of Welfare acknowledged in 1936 that neither private nor public agencies had provided adequately "for the colored child, who is out of step in the march of life," thus placing more onus on the child than the community. In 1939, only four voluntary agencies in New York accepted black children for placement in segregated and inferior institutions. Only one institution (with 26 beds) accepted both black and white children.[4] The public department would not "interfere" with voluntary agency policies or practices. When questioned in court, a black probation officer explained his failure to secure foster home care for two small, orphaned children: "Every door of placement is shut down, and that is what faces us at this time." Endless excuses were given to the court for not accepting black children: limited places must be kept for children who would make the best use of them; agencies could only work with cooperative families; social agencies could not deal with generalized family pathology; they could not work with primitive parents, incapable of conceptual thinking.

Denials of services were couched in condescending terms. A plea by Reverend Shelton Hale Bishop, the distinguished black Episcopalian minister of St. Philip's Church, for acceptance of black children in 1941 was rejected by the most prestigious Protestant agencies. The president of one agency wrote that the board had considered his request, but had decided that the time had not come for such changes, and hoped that Reverend Bishop would understand.[5] Another sectarian agency agreed to accept a small black child for foster home care but only on the condition that the mother, of darker complexion, would not visit the child who could "pass." This agency was outraged by my refusal to agree to such a condition for care. Rather than accept black children for care, some voluntary agencies invited a token black to join their boards as window dressing.

In the few institutions that accepted black children, they were often segregated and given inferior training. As their vocational assignments, black boys were assigned to unskilled maintenance work and black girls were assigned to work in the laundry. On one institutional visit, a director explained to me that black girls had greater sexual problems, lower IQs, and that they liked to work in the steam laundry. The denial of foster home care for black children was based on three other myths: that there were no good black foster homes; that there were no competent black social workers; and that black children could only be placed in black foster homes. These myths persisted long after a 1941 demonstration, supported by Marshall Field. The interracial staff, directed by a black supervisor, had successfully placed more than 150 black children in foster homes.[6]

In 1936, when a 10-year-old black boy ran away from a miserable home situation to sleep on rooftops and to beg food for survival, he was charged with juvenile delinquency. Probation advised that the Juvenile Court could do nothing for him until he committed a felony or became 12 and could be sent to the State School for delinquents. I took 20 such cases to Mayor La-Guardia. Shocked by the exclusion of young, black children from care, the Mayor called the Episcopal Bishop of New York, who turned for help to the Protestant Episcopal Mission Society. They agreed to set up a summer camp for black youngsters. The Camp did well and became the Wiltwyck School for Boys, the first agency in the East to accept neglected and delinquent black boys between 8 and 12 years of age, without regard to religion.

Until 1942, Wiltwyck was under the direction of Protestant ministers appointed by the Mission Society. Marshall Field, who visited the school and saw its inadequate plant and staff, provided a school and professional staff with the understanding the Mission would absorb the operating costs over a period of years. However, when World War II came, the Mission Society decided to concentrate on preparing chaplains for the armed services. To avoid the closing of the only residential resource for young neglected and delinquent black children, a new board composed of the Minister of the Riverside Church, a few Juvenile Court judges, some social workers and mental health professionals was established. It was nonsectarian and interracial. Marion Anderson provided the necessary mortgage funds through Judge Delany. Wiltwyck placed stress on social work, mental health services, arts, crafts, and education. Mrs. Roosevelt joined the new board and found time to visit the school and have the children come for picnics at Hyde Park. President Roosevelt was enlisted to read stories to the children at Christmas time, an event so exciting that they did not want to go on home visits.

The Ongoing Tolerance of Racism

After an antidiscriminative local law was enacted in 1941 by the City Council and after the city was notified that Wiltwyck was open to children regardless of race, the Department of Welfare began slowly and hesitantly to refer some white boys to Wiltwyck.

In 1949, a remarkable social worker, Ernst Papanek, was chosen as director. He had collected and worked with the lost children in Vienna for many years. When Hitler came to power, he escaped with a group of Jewish children and led them across Europe to Spain and safety. On coming to this country, he chose to work with black and other minority children, whom he saw as the most deprived. He abhorred traditional punishments and tried to replace them by teaching children the consequences of wrongful behavior.

Years later when hundreds of records were reviewed, it was found that many youths who had done well at Wiltwyck reverted to delinquency when they were returned to their former homes and the city ghettoes. There were, however, noteworthy exceptions, including Claude Brown, author of *Manchild in the Promised Land*, and Floyd Patterson, who became the world's heavyweight champion. They looked on Wiltwyck as home, and on Papanek as a father. Floyd Patterson returned to the campus to teach the boys how to box, and he gave part of his winnings to establish an early halfway home in New York City for children ready for discharge. He recalled boys who could not go home because they had no homes to which they could return.

The case history of Wiltwyck, like that of its children, was one of many hardships, including a constant lack of funds and confrontation with hostile neighbors who used zoning laws to keep them out. A series of financial crises and renewed community hostility finally forced it to close in 1983. Its major achievement, aid to individual children, was its demonstration that, under a nonsectarian and interracial board black children could be integrated into interracial child-care facilities, and be helped by treatment and good care.

Within the Juvenile Court, neither the victims of racial discrimination nor those who enforced it paid much heed. Parents were unaware of how far discrimination limited the services their children received. They were not told why their children were rejected for care and held in shelters while white children were leap-frogged into the "better facilities." There were few lawyers to question discriminatory treatment. There was little discussion among the judges about how to overcome racial discrimination, and it was not mentioned to children or parents brought before the court. Even judges opposed to discrimination and willing to beat the bushes for an individual child, yielded to the pervasive controls imposed by institutional racism. When there was no voluntary agency willing to accept a neglected child and no home to which the child could be returned, a flimsy delinquency petition might be concocted in order to get a bed for a black child in the State Training School for delinquents.

In the North as in the South, the interpretation of *Plessy* allowed and invited separate and inferior services for black children everywhere from 1890 to the 1960s. Throughout the country, institutions for delinquent black boys and girls were found so desolate and forbidding as to threaten their lives.[7] When voluntary agencies were given responsibility for nonwhite children, a scattering of poor, segregated, and insufficient services remained the main resources for the Juvenile Court.

Tolerance of institutional racism was deeply entrenched in the child-care world. After summing up other inadequacies of the temporary care system, the Chairman of the New York Welfare Council referred to noncompliance with the City resolution against discrimination as "irritating."

Role of Voluntary Agencies

Tolerance of racial discrimination allowed voluntary agencies to avoid responsibility not only for residential care but also for preventive services for nonwhite children in the community. A random sampling in the 1940s of 500 families in one Harlem public school with a high delinquency rate revealed that not a single child was known to any voluntary agency during the preceding 2 years.[8]

As early as 1940, Judge Dudley Sicher wrote to his colleagues that, "The placement of Negro children has become such a cruelly baffling problem as to call for some affirmative action by our board." He suggested that publicly supported charitable agencies be required to accept black children, but no action was taken. This position was partially incorporated a year later, in the first local legislation prohibiting City reimbursement to any agency refusing a "reasonable proportion" of children because of race or color.[9]

Although the Catholic and Jewish agencies offered to comply with the new law, the Commissioner of Welfare reported strong opposition among Protestant agencies to caring for white and black children in the same institution.[10] Delays in compliance and excuses were many. One agency chairman piously proclaimed that his board did not believe in keeping records on "the percentage of any ethnic group, white or black." Some admitted black children to black foster homes but not to their institutions. Others accepted only token numbers. The "threshold of tolerance" was introduced as a new guideline. Secret quotas were introduced. When a worker in court explained rejection of a black child because the quota had been filled, her supervisor quickly denied that the rejection had anything to do with race. Six years after the enactment of the local antidiscrimination law, only token compliance had been achieved.[11]

Professionals also played a role in obstructing the antidiscrimination law. Some social workers would explain they were not responsible for rejections of black children because they only implemented policy decisions made by their boards. A bigoted judge exclaimed, "God put the colored people in Africa. He did not mean to mix them with whites. I pass Jamaica Bay as I drive home. I see the black ducks in the water and the white seagulls in the sky. They don't mix. Why should we mix the children?"

City and State Agencies Avoid Responsibility

Voluntary agencies were not alone in tolerating and engaging in institutional racism. In New York City, both city and state government agencies condoned it by failing to address the consequences for black children. Although the voluntary agencies claimed that they did not discriminate, an official report on the need for 1,100 additional residential places stated that a study of cases (March 1947 to April 1948) showed that only 42% of the children placed had received the type of care indicated by good child-care standards.[12] A high proportion were black. Still, the representatives of the voluntary agencies and the City reached no agreement on the development of long-term services. Black children, held at the public shelter, waited as long as 2 years while voluntary agencies refused to commit themselves to the numbers of black children they would accept.

The first moral break in this deadlock situation came from a 1946 resolution by the Commission on Christian Social Ethics of the Episcopal Church under the leadership of Reverend Leland Henry: "In view of the failure of the sectarian agencies to meet the needs of dependent and neglected children in the City, the Department of Welfare...should accept responsibility with adequate provision for religious instruction."[13] The Protestant Federation objected and the City remained quiescent.

Cautious Movement Toward Public Services

After further reports from the court, citizen groups and the Department of Welfare on the lack of facilities for black children, the Mayor approved in February 1949 a modest plan for the Department of Welfare to initiate its own foster home program. Delays followed and the Department agreed to limit its program to Protestant black children. The City Commissioner reported to the state again in 1953 on the critical needs of black and Puerto Rican children both in their homes and in temporary care. But neither City nor state would challenge the adamant opposition by the voluntary agencies to an increase in public services.

A City Subterfuge for Services to Black Children

The City's answer in 1956 was to create a fictitious private agency, to be administered by Mayoral appointees selected from the three major faiths, on land bought by the City and with its budget to be paid 100% by the City. The result of this subterfuge was the creation of Hillcrest, a place of last resort for dependent and neglected children who had been rejected by all voluntary agencies. By 1964, of 200 children there, only 4 were white.[14] The Director told me that on those rare occasions when a white child was referred, "I know that child will be climbing the wall." This institution in New York temporarily reduced the embarrassment to the City and voluntary agencies resulting from their rejection of black children. But black children received only inferior services in a *de facto*, northern, segregated institution.

At a Foster Care Commission meeting in 1959, a breakdown of the number of children awaiting placement showed that of 852 such children, 435 were black and 122 were Puerto Rican—a total of 557 or 65% non-white. At this point, Judge Delany and I moved for the establishment of a public service by the Welfare Department for children whom voluntary agencies could not or would not accept promptly, but our proposal was blasted as "communistic and totalitarian" by a judge acting as emissary from the Cardinal.

Despite denials of discrimination, the number of nonwhite babies held in hospital wards had continued to increase. In July 1959, the Deputy Mayor told my husband and me that the situation was so critical that the City was planning to reopen a ward in a defunct tuberculosis hospital for care of these babies.

During a sleepless night, the thought came that if the City would compensate mothers on AFDC for boarding an infant, good homes could be found, babies would get personal care, welfare families could be raised above the poverty level, and AFDC mothers would have a new sense of self-worth. The next day I spoke to New York State Commissioner Houston, who replied that if the City would do anything so sensible it would find the state cooperative. That afternoon after court, I took the proposal to the City Commissioner. At first he hesitated, invoking a social work principle that no foster home should be used where financial support was necessary. Shooting from the hip, I retorted that then he should close all the voluntary agencies that depended on the City for 80% to 90% of their budgets. He answered, "You're very tough!" and laughed. He embarked on a 3-year project,[15] and within months he reported on the benefits to children with AFDC mothers and on savings to the City. The project director described the babies transferred from hospitals to the AFDC foster homes as "beginning to bloom."[16] For reasons never explained, the project never became an ongoing part of the work of the public department.

Discrimination Continued by City and Voluntary Agencies

In 1962, racial discrimination in New York was still rampant, despite all the protestations about constitutional rights. When I checked on 56 children held in congregate shelter for more than 1 year awaiting placement, the records showed 45 were black, 4 were Puerto Rican, and 3 were Eurasian.

City officials claimed they did not have racial data on children in need of placement and concealed what information they had. At the same time, their staff required detailed racial information from probation officers on black and Puerto Rican children before accepting them for emergency or temporary care. One black probation officer protested that "allocation workers (in the Department of Welfare) must know the exact shade or coloring of a child: light, brown, dark or black, and if the hair is coarse or straight. [They] ask, 'Does the child have Negroid features?'"[17] When this practice was brought to the attention of Commissioner Mitchell Ginsberg, he ordered that it be stopped. But it was renewed again after he left office.

As late as 1962, the City continued to justify discrimination by voluntary agencies. When questioned as to why an abandoned infant had been left in a congregate shelter for more than a year, the City Department worker replied, "He is a fair skinned child with a broad nose, and kinky black hair, evidently the product of an interracial couple." On walking into chambers in July 1971, during my last year on the bench, I overheard a probation officer say, "Yes, he is Negro, but a beautiful little boy. I cannot say he is light skinned, but he is beautiful." I took the phone to ask the reasons for such questions. The answer was, "I am following regular procedure."

In December 1973, the desks in the City's Special Services for Children were still separated by religion and by whether staff was serving white, black, or Puerto Rican children. Finally, on September 25, 1974, Commissioner James Dumpson issued a statement, entitled "Revised Changes in Policy and Probation Procedures Regarding Placement of Children with Special Needs." Expressing concern for approximately 2,000 children with special needs for whom no placements in voluntary agencies was available, this overdue statement set forth that the best interests of the child must be paramount over any other consideration. However, it added that "Every effort will be made in each case where practicable, to protect the religious heritage of the child."

Six months later, on March 31, 1975, when a task force met with the Welfare staff, we were told that in the system of allocation, "Religion naturally comes first."

Racial Quotas Outlawed

It was not until 1974 that the City officially outlawed quotas based on race, and required voluntary agencies to report all vacancies to the public department. It took an act of courage by an assistant administrator, Carol Parry, to write that referrals of "hard-to-place" children would be assigned simultaneously to all appropriate agencies.[18] At about this time on a visit to the public shelters, I found that two-thirds of the children were black, 30% were Puerto Rican and less than 5% were white.

State and Courts Move with Deliberate Delay

New York State administrators, like those in the City, avoided the issue of racial discrimination as long as possible. State investigation reports on the voluntary agencies did not challenge racial segregation or the exclusion of children by voluntary agencies for racial reasons. The state also failed to encourage the establishment of public services although desperately needed for nonwhite children. It ignored or misinterpreted the State constitutional mandate "to provide for any destitute child who cannot be properly cared for in his home."[19]

Juvenile Court judges, trained to follow precedent, inhaled the anesthesia of neutrality when confronted by social injustice. While pursuing justice in individual cases, this anesthesia was reinforced by Appellate Courts that regarded Constitutional questions as their prerogatives and beyond the scope or competence of inferior court judges.

Changing Black Attitudes

Changing attitudes among black parents toward their children and the Juvenile Court had begun to appear in the 1950s. Parents of adolescents charged with school misconduct, fighting with white boys, or stealing from white-owned stores assured judges that they would see that their sons behaved if allowed to return home. But, one could also sense an unspoken pride that their sons had stood up to "the man" as they had never dared to do. Their pride was different from the teachings of a small organization, "the five percenters," which preached that black youths should attack whites wherever they found them, and, also, attack blacks who served whites. One 13-year-old black boy who had attacked an elderly white couple without cause announced in court that the world was composed of 85% whites who oppressed blacks, 10% Uncle Toms, and the 5 percenters, under the leadership of Allah, to whom the world would belong. A 15-year-old, who had assaulted a black errand boy and taken his money, gave an Arabic name and claimed he had no parents and that he wanted no part of blacks who were Uncle Toms. His saddened parents stood by bewildered.

In this period also, black professionals began to show open resentment of the long stays for black children in shelters, the denial of adoption, and the failure of child care agencies to work with black families toward a child's return home. They resented what they saw as insulting and excessive policing of blacks dependent on welfare. In time, resentments hardened so that a group of black social workers saw a separate professional organization as the only remedy for unequal treatment.

The 1960s: Promises to Keep

The Juvenile Court Law of 1962 required review of all children in placement over 18 months.[20] Judges could then see what actually happened to nonwhite children for whom placement had been ordered, even when agencies tried to avoid criticism of what they had done or failed to do.

These reviews repeatedly revealed institutional racism: Ellen was an abandoned 4-year-old of superior beauty and intelligence, but not considered for adoption because of her "dark coloring."[21] The Department of Welfare had approved continuing foster care for Martin, a superior, attractive infant, because the chances of adoption were "slim for Negro and Puerto Rican children." Some agency representatives still claimed that foster care could provide all a child needed, if the child was nonwhite.

A new phrase was coined to explain or justify the failure to secure appropriate care or placement. "Hard-to-place children" was the euphemism, which continues to this day, to explain or conceal the reasons for rejecting children with special physical or mental disabilities, and nonwhite children.

When I insisted that an attractive 3-year-old, abandoned by her parents, should be considered for adoption, the Department of Welfare supported the voluntary agency position that adoptive planning was "neither realistic nor feasible." Because she was Catholic and black, no adoption agency would consider her. Some refused on the basis of religion, while others claimed they had no black homes. Still others stated they could not act contrary to the wishes of the agency that had been given custody by the Department of Welfare. This "hard-to-place" child was denied an adoptive home.

Puerto Ricans: Target for Discrimination

Although the United States had granted citizenship to Puerto Ricans in 1917, they were made the targets of vicious attacks in the 1950s. By 1959, of the 650,000 Puerto Ricans in New York City, only 25% had been born on the mainland and a large proportion of these were children. Although an unknown number belonged to evangelical sects, it was generally assumed that Puerto Ricans were Catholic. Catholic agencies were as ill- prepared to meet the needs of these children as the Protestant agencies had been to meet the needs of black children who came North in large numbers after World War I. Limited by religious matching and prejudice, non-Catholic agencies showed little concern for Puerto Rican children.

Puerto Ricans, like previous newcomers to this country, were held responsible for the rise in crime and delinquency. One New York Supreme Court judge, ignoring their rights as citizens, proposed that they be deported to save welfare costs. Child-care agencies drew new color lines. They demanded that the Juvenile Court report whether children, and even infants, were "light" or "dark" Puerto Rican. These differences were noted on official court papers. One mother, about to be hospitalized, was advised that her three children would have to be placed separately, because one was "light," one was "mulatto," and one was "olive skinned." The excuse for not referring a 3-year-old Puerto Rican child for adoption was masqueraded as "necessary to find a family similar in coloring, cultural descent and genetic origin"!

The enactment by Congress of the Civil Rights Act of 1964 brought great promise. Its passage represented a high point in the conscience of the American people as well as Federal law:

No person in the United States shall on the grounds of race, color or national origin, be excluded from participating in or be denied the benefits of, or be subjected to discrimination under any program or activity receiving Federal financial assistance.[22]

These were brave words. They promised an end to the successive attacks on newcomers that had affected the Irish, the Jews, the Italians, the Chinese, and the Japanese. They established a new ideal for conduct toward black and Puerto Rican children in America.

Nevertheless, in western states, children of Spanish-speaking families continued to be subjected to harsh discrimination in schools. An HEW investigator found that 90% of the children not promoted in one area of California had Spanish surnames.[23] Chicano children were subjected to many humiliations. In one school, a teacher stood in the doorway and sprayed Chicano children with perfume before she permitted their admission. A first-grade little girl was made to stand in the corner for saying in Spanish, "I don't understand." In a drawing class when a child said he had no crayons, the teacher snapped, "If your father got off welfare and went to work, you'd have crayons."[24] The disparity in educational achievement compared to that of white children grew wider with each year in school as it had done between black and white children years earlier in New York. Special education became a new instrument for holding nonwhite children in classes for slow learners.

Spanish-speaking parents were accused of having too little interest in the education of their children. But, when workers in New York's Bank Street College of Education made home visits, they learned that the mothers cared far more than the schools recognized. Visits were welcomed by mothers eager to hear about how their children were doing in school. They spoke with sadness of not being able to go to school and meet the teachers. They explained they could not speak English, that they had no decent clothes, and that their children were ashamed to have them go to schools or meet their teachers.

Juvenile Court Judges and Racial Discrimination

Faced each day with children for whom the judges could do little or nothing, a few of us met back in July 1938 and decided to gather the facts on services for "colored children." Probation had reported that the four main services for even segregated placement had closed intake,[25] while the number of black children brought before the court had continued to rise dramatically. In 1940, a Court Committee on Institutions found the situation "hopeless." [26] Visits by judges to institutions for delinquent children, to state schools, to schools for the mentally retarded, and to treatment facilities showed that the degree of custodial restrictions and lack of treatment services rose directly with the proportion of nonwhite children.

Continuing reports by the court to Mayors, the Department of Welfare, and voluntary agencies on lack of services for black children had brought only minute improvements. Judges could beg voluntary agencies to accept nonwhite children, but they had no power to command help. Judges were expected to do their best within the law, and not take issue with "the law." There was no discussion of racism except among a few close colleagues. Most judges were polite and silent at ceremonial meetings with the boards of social agencies, which remained 99% white. The boards maintained a tone of aloof benevolence toward judges, but showed little concern for the needs of nonwhite children.

Traditional institutional racism continued through the 1960s. Agencies requested extensions of placement for black children even when the only hope for a permanent home was through adoption, and the judges were all too compliant. As doorways from institutions to foster homes came last for nonwhite children, so too their adoptive placements in homes came slowly and last.

In New York, it was only in 1972, after an interprofessional committee, appointed by New York's Appellate Division, publicized its findings on serious racial discrimination, that the voluntary agencies showed concern. A sampling of delinquent and PINS youths in 1970 and 1971 had revealed that the voluntary agencies accepted 78% of those who were white, but only 24% of the black and 34% of the Puerto Rican children referred for placement by the Juvenile Court. Seriously disturbed children had been sent to the State Training Schools, which had practically no treatment services, while the private residential treatment agencies that received higher levels of payment from the state accepted only less delinquent and less disturbed children.[27,28]

Following publication of the report, three sectarian federations invited me, as Chairman of the Committee, and Elizabeth Schack, the Project Director, to a meeting. All the agency executives were white. When a black professor of social work entered the room she asked, with forced humor, whether she had been invited by the voluntary agencies to add color to the conclave. There was no indication of a readiness to change discriminatory patterns. Instead, only excuses and justifications for discriminatory practices were voiced.

Seven years later, a group of mental health professionals found a similar pattern of racism in Connecticut. Asked by the Juvenile Court in New Haven to study the more serious delinquents, the professionals reported that black delinquents were disproportionately denied treatment services and assigned to correctional agencies. The study questioned the ability of professionals to identify severe pathology in the black community. It asked why neglect and abuse in black families were more easily overlooked than in white families. It noted that pathological behavior of psychiatrically impaired black patients was too often dismissed as an ethnic characteristic. Instead of psychotic, the less demanding label of *primitive thinking* was more often assigned to blacks. Extreme grandiosity was taken as street bravado and bizarre behavior was interpreted to be manipulation.[29]

Of the many cases during all my years on the bench, two involving institutional racism stand out in memory. One involved racism in the public school system; the other, racism in welfare. Both involved wrongs to individual children condoned by officialdom. In 1958, 4 years after *Brown*, the New York City Board of Education filed a neglect petition against two sets of parents who refused to register their 12- and 13-year-old children in junior high schools to which they had been assigned. These parents admitted their refusal, but contended that the assignment of their children to segregated and inferior schools violated the guarantee of equal protection under the 14th Amendment. The City contended the parents had not exhausted procedural remedies and that the Juvenile Court should not consider the constitutional issue. After overruling the City's objections, the trial focused on whether the schools to which the children had been assigned were, in fact, segregated and inferior as compared to those where white children predominated.

The two junior high schools were, indeed, the only ones in the City where the student population was all black and Puerto Rican; the teachers were less qualified than in schools where children were predominantly white; there were more substitutes and fewer licensed teachers; the vacancies in positions had reached more than 50%; and the Board of Education was still permitting all but novices to choose where they preferred to teach. After extensive hearings, I held that the "Board of Education has no moral

or legal right to ask that this court shall punish parents, or deprive them of
the custody of their children for refusal to accept an unconstitutional condition in the schools to which the Board assigned their children....The defen-
ses on ground of inferior educational opportunities in these schools by
reason of racial discrimination...bar(s) an adjudication of neglect." The petition of neglect was dismissed.[30]

Controversy followed, but the City did not pursue its notice of appeal.
The black press and community groups hailed the decision as the first northern decision against *de facto* segregation in the public schools. Hate mail,
generally anonymous, arrived in volume. Fourteen years later, I received
the last vituperative letter: "People like you are the real criminals—not the
stupid black and white niggers who are wrecking a once great City and nation. They are doing what scum like you have taught them to do—take an
aggressive violent stance or demand their alleged rights. May you rot in
hell." The return address was given as Smolensk, U.S.S.R.

Racism in Child Welfare

Racism in the court reflected the widespread racism throughout child
welfare. Shirley's mother had died when Shirley was 3, and her
grandmother when the child was 11. Her father took her into his home where
she was made to feel unwanted by a proverbial stepmother, who scolded
and beat her by turns. After running away and begging forgiveness on
several occasions, Shirley was brought to court by the father. He wanted
her "put away."

At that time, Shirley was a small, attractive girl with a mischievous
smile. She begged for a "home." The psychiatrist reported normal intelligence, no signs of psychosis, but need for residential treatment to help her
work out deep feelings of loss and abandonment. For 10 months the court
tried to find such a placement in Protestant, Catholic, Jewish, and nonsectarian agencies. But there were only rejections for this Protestant black child.
She was shunted between her father's home, shelters, and detention; she became defiant when her father stopped visiting her. A year after her father
had first brought her to court, she asked in a near whisper, "Is my father
here?" The answer was again "No." She tried to look as though it did not
matter.

With no placement available in any voluntary agency, I felt forced to place Shirley in the New York State Training School. After making this miserable decision, I asked the law guardian who represented her whether the time had not come for a class action against the agencies that had rejected this homeless child. Subsequently, the Legal Aid Society and the New York Civil Liberties Union commenced a class action against the City and all voluntary children's agencies, charging violations of the Constitutional rights of Protestant, black children.[31] Catholic Charities and the Federation of Jewish Philanthropies asserted the right of voluntary agencies under sectarian sponsorship to maintain preferential admission policies favoring children of their faiths. The Protestant Federation, which had done most in recent years for nonwhite children,[32] after serious internal debate, filed a brief in support of the action. It disapproved preferential admissions on the basis of religion that resulted in inferior and unequal treatment for Protestant black children. A few of its member organizations disagreed and withdrew from the Federation. Within the Jewish Federation there were also conflicting views, but a large majority of the trustees voted to support the defendants. When I opposed this position, Federation asked me to resign as its representative on the Human Resources Advisory Committee.

Since 1972 the case has been dragged through the courts while a series of Federal judges postponed trials. The issue before the present court is limited to whether the New York law, in its application, results in racial and religious discrimination.[33] Settlement talks have continued on with endless delays. Nevertheless, the *Wilder* case has shown the value of class actions that strike at racial discrimination. Juvenile Court judges reported that after it was filed, new openings appeared and increased among agencies formerly closed or nearly closed to nonwhite children.

Finally, in the fall of 1986, Federal District Court Judge Robert Ward issued a landmark decision for a proposed settlement.[34] It directed the end of racial or religious discrimination in the acceptance of children by tax-supported child-care agencies. Hopefully, like *Brown v. Board of Education* in the field of public education, this decision in *Wilder* will, eventually, create equal opportunities for all children in the child-care field.

Progress toward less racism was spurred on by demographic shifts that made it necessary for all residential agencies to accept more nonwhite children of different faiths or close their facilities. Beds had to be filled for economic reasons and there were fewer and fewer white children to fill them in New York.

Discriminatory Thorns Among the 1970 Reforms

Civil libertarians, intent on restricting what they regarded as arbitrary use of judicial discretion and on reducing Juvenile Court intervention, pressed hard for separating status offenders from juvenile delinquents. They did not realize that this "reform" would be abused by its application to nonwhite youth. They did not recognize that white youths would be more likely to be designated as "persons in need of supervision," or PINS, and referred for treatment, while black youth would be more likely to be designated as delinquents for similar offenses and sent to correctional institutions.

In 1979, the Federal government reported that 86% of the children in public facilities had been found delinquent, and only 14% were not found delinquent (11% status offenders and 3% nonoffenders). In contrast, in the private agencies, only 32% were found delinquent, whereas 68% were not found delinquent (of these, 26% were status offenders and 42% were neglected, abused, or mentally ill children). A similar disparity was found in a 1979 LEAA report that showed that, although black children comprised one-third of the population in public agencies, they comprised only one-fifth of the population in voluntary agencies.[35]

In the 1970s, when civil rights were on the popular agenda, discrimination took new and devious forms. In 1971, one experienced teacher and practitioner in child care wrote about new methods used by voluntary agencies to exclude nonwhite children: they imposed alien foods; they failed to provide equal access to religious observance; they insisted on their own religious ambiance; and they issued unwritten warnings that there would be a decline in white referrals if too many black children or black staff were accepted. Compliance with laws or regulations in support of affirmative action was half-hearted.

As new state codes allowed waivers of youths from the Juvenile Courts to the Criminal Courts at a younger age and for a wider number of offenses, nonwhite children became the obvious objects for discrimination. The first photographs of youth being fingerprinted on their way to jail under New York's 1978 Juvenile Offender Law showed only black faces. One reporter described them as "young faces masking very old lives" with the youths appearing confused, afraid, and lonely.[36]

Black and White Responses to Racism

At lunch one day, one black judge said to another black judge, "When I have a colored boy free and able to go to school, but playing hookey, I throw the book at him. I won't sit by while he throws away what we worked so hard to get." The second and younger black judge replied in a gentle voice, "They don't really know they're free yet. They don't know or believe that schools will bring them freedom or a different life. I try to tell them, but I can't blame them for not believing."

Teachers, social workers, child-care agencies, and the public departments have all told judges over the years what should or could be done for individual children. They often did not seem to realize how what they said affected children's feelings about themselves. In court, professionals and nonprofessionals often lowered their voices, as though black parents and children would not hear or understand their prejudicial words. Over and over again I wanted to halt the procedure and to recite a poem by Countee Cullen:

> Once riding in old Baltimore
> Heart filled, head filled with glee
> I saw a Baltimorean keep
> Looking straight at me.
> Now I was eight and very small
> And he was no whit bigger
> And so I smiled, but he poked out
> His tongue and called me "Nigger."
> I saw the whole of Baltimore
> From May until December.
> Of all the things that happened there
> That's all that I remember.

Many whites who initially were eager to correct racial discrimination through affirmative action lost their zeal and claim this task is completed. They became moralistic in their judgments of blacks, demanding "the postponement of present satisfactions so that youth would become future-oriented." They did not see how past injuries have seared the lives of more than one generation. In the Juvenile Court such injuries appeared vividly when two parents begged for help for their 12-year-old son who would not speak. Bellevue Hospital reported that the boy did not believe his father was his real father because his father and siblings were of lighter color and called him a Negro. He spoke of the wish to kill his father and his brothers and sisters, who regarded themselves as white. He thought frequently of suicide. The hospital report concluded "The symptoms which he has are not considered as pathological as if they had occurred in a white boy ... he is miserably preoccupied with his color. It is possible that he is having only a temporary psychosis associated with the problems he is facing at puberty."

White adults are often blind to how they hurt black children. On a visit to one segregated institution, the Director proudly displayed beautiful grounds where no children played and a gracious reception room for guests. The subdued behavior of the delinquent girls reflected the stern controls that governed their lives. At lunch in the well-appointed apartment of the Director, a black girl waited on table. After lunch, the Director said with obvious self-approval, "That is a lovely and competent girl. I have told her that though her skin is black, her soul can be white."

It has become fashionable of late to deplore affirmative action as either reverse discrimination or as no longer needed. Yet, so far as black youths are concerned, affirmative action has touched only the tip of surrounding icebergs. The price for years of racism cannot be paid by a few, short years of affirmative action. In his more than 15 years of effective achievements in the New Haven schools, Dr. James Comer has shown what can be done with skill, infinite patience, and high expectations for children, to improve academic achievement and the behavior of ghetto children. Parents and teachers have been involved in this program. Comer has also demonstrated that no quick fix will overcome "centuries' old injuries" and restore self-esteem.

The increase in the number of black children born out of wedlock has caused anguish in the black community and aroused anger in the general community. By 1985, 57% of black infants were born out of wedlock. Many programs to reduce pregnancy among unmarried black adolescents have proliferated, but programs that allow young mothers to live with their infants remain all but nonexistent. Most important, training programs leading to jobs for youth in the ghettos have all but disappeared since the 1980s, so that today few young black males can afford to marry or provide for a child. The shortage of economically stable young men was recently described with bitter humor as the shrinkage of the MMPI. These letters stood for the "marriageable male population index." Although unemployment of blacks remains twice that for whites, "immorality" and "welfare" are still singled out as the two causes for the high rate of illegitimacy in the black community.

Sparks of conscience in the larger community and anger among those left out from American prosperity must eventually light or relight different responses. Then the current battles over affirmative action will appear only as a skirmish or delaying tactic in the long war to end racial injustice.

At a symposium in the winter of 1978, a great Federal judge, J. Skelley Wright, after paying tribute to the significance of *Brown v. Board of Education*, stated, "But when we shall move again in dramatic fashion—that is a much more troublesome question."[37]

Chapter 11
Postscript for the Future

Born of generous impulses, justice for youth was flawed from the outset. It never became a parent of wanted children to whom generous sharing is the greatest joy. It was too closely modeled on charity that granted only what could be spared. Youths before the Court remained other people's children. Justice for them was treated as an object for basement bargaining or viewed as a luxury item within the larger system of criminal justice. Juvenile Courts, like the youths before them, became the proverbial step-children of American justice. High-sounding legislation was not translated into resources that required a redistribution of community wealth or a challenge to religious separatism or racial discrimination. Black, Puerto Rican, and Spanish-speaking youth were continuously excluded from services, regardless of religious affiliation.

When troubled youth were perceived as newcomers, strangers, or the children of failed parents, the call to meet their needs lost vigor. Minority youth living in poverty were regarded as a threat to order. Like children, disavowed by disappointed parents, the blame for misconduct was displaced entirely to the youth. Society was advised to do less and less. The urge to make them disappear (at least temporarily) through reincarceration was cloaked as "just deserts" in the 1970s.

Judges, confronting heavier caseloads without benefit of added resources, were drawn toward blindness to the needs and potentialities of individual children. Confidence in the purpose of their work was undermined. Although they still struggled to pull rabbits out of a mess of hats for a few children, forgetfulness of the many others provided an opiate for survival. Addiction to this opiate prepared the way for yielding to the harsh demands for more and more punishment in the 1980s. The alleged cost saving through more criminalization ignored the costs to youths.

In this debilitating process that sapped the conscience of the judiciary, the media often acted like Monday morning quarterbacks. They swung from occasional compassion to frequent denunciations of too-lenient punishments. There was little regard for the responsibility of judges to make independent and impartial decisions in every case.

Without excusing or justifying the stance of judges or the media, the Juvenile Courts were also subject to a diminished concept of justice for youth. Old allies who had rendered direct services had been thrust aside as intermeddlers who engaged in questionable hands-on good works. Their contributions had not achieved equal justice, but they had provided human relationships as an integral part of the Juvenile Court system beyond that existing in other courts. They were replaced by staffs of bureaucracies who had insufficient time, skills, or commitment to reach out to troubled youths. Distancing, welcomed in the name of procedural due process, became the primary concern in the courts, as well as in other institutions, including schools and health services.

The lessening concern for youths who lived in and would be returned to lives of poverty in deprived areas played a dominant role in the decline of juvenile justice. Politicians responded to raised voices demanding that the Juvenile Courts protect them from the depredations of delinquent youth. State laws were enacted to require judges to determine which delinquent youth would, in the future, engage in serious delinquent acts. Judges were required to undertake the impossible assignment of predicting which youths would recidivate or be "dangerous" if returned to the community. Longer and fixed terms of incarceration were to be based on judicial predictions of potential dangerousness.

Heavy Hands of Poverty

Draconian measures against delinquent youth were not accompanied by serious efforts to address or redress the causes of their poverty or their alienation from the community. Old and new myths were invoked to explain growing poverty in the country. False myths exaggerated the concentration of poverty in central cities and the preponderance of nonwhite among the dependent poor. False myths were spread about the increase of unmarried mothers in the nonwhite community without acknowledgment of the faster increase in the white community. Moralistic judgments of unmarried mothers made the prevention of adolescent pregnancy a favored project, without confronting the poverty or conditions of life that lead to such pregnancies. It was urged that unmarried mothers be required to work full time, even while their children were still under 6, 3, and even less than a year, if the mothers were dependent on public welfare. These demands contrast with the practice of married women with small children, only 27% of whom worked full time.

Reducing the numbers of those dependent on public welfare became the major objective of public policy. Even recent reports on improving public welfare are caught up in the numbers game, and how to put those remaining on welfare to work. Confronting the causes of increased poverty is subordinated to recommendations for "incremental" improvements as all that can be expected in the near future. How to stay or reverse the decline in wages for the working poor, to raise the outdated minimum wage, or develop training and work programs for poor youth are questions postponed for another day. Serious warnings that the earlier and more protracted adolescence of youth requires early action if current behavior problems of youth are to be corrected before they are "cast in concrete" have received little response.

The Reagan administration continues to grind out only more devices for relegating federal responsibility for the poor, including unemployed youth, to the states and localities. It encourages the lapse of standards for aid regulated by Congress. An ethos of boredom with the problems of the poor has spread. Despite rhetoric about the importance of "the family," little interest is shown in what can be done for poor parents and their children.

Postscript for the Future

The search for greater justice for youth stands at a dangerous crossroad. Confronted by widespread hostility toward nonconforming youth, there are also hopeful signs of new knowledge and growing concern on the part of those seeking to place public welfare above private interests.

Generous prescriptions for the treatment of youth and demands for harsh punishment have alternated in the United States as in other lands. They have reflected and followed periods of general optimism or pessimism toward the future. In this country we are, hopefully, approaching the end of a mean period during which the well-being of youth, the poor, and minority groups has been treated as unimportant or beyond reach. We have witnessed how saving costs in human services has fallen most heavily on the most vulnerable members of society. The rationing of justice, like the rationing of health, has fostered neglect and violence.

Observation of the administration of juvenile justice during the past 50 years throws light on periods of progress, periods of marking time, and a steady distancing from youth during the past decade. As in other fields there has been a loss of ardor, imagination, and commitment to youth, and especially to poor youth. This does not mean that this country cannot address the problems of troubled or troubling youth. It does, however, mean that neither a return to past ways, nor the acceptance of what passes as juvenile justice today, will suffice.

Many institutions for youth have endured beyond their usefulness. It is easier to mock the efforts of long ago—the workhouses, the asylums, the orphanages, and the orphan trains—than to confront present practices. Today, the lack of trust between parents and children, and the community's aggressive demands for protection, contribute to an avoidance of facing the consequences of increasing poverty and declining confidence in the future by the young.

Tasks for the Juvenile Courts Today

When America again moves toward more generous programs for its youth, Juvenile Courts will have a special role to play. They are witness to the consequences of failed policies and practices hurtful to youth. They are in a position to present what they see as constant cases of injuries to youth. They can look beyond individual cases to discover patterns of wrongful injuries to youth, whether inflicted by communities, agencies, or parental failures.

At the same time, the Juvenile Courts must pursue the daily task of trying youth and making decisions for their future. They must pick up the pieces for individual youths and parents that have been allowed to fall through the cracks of institutions. They must act as sentinels to protect youth against both overreaching and underdoing on the part of those charged by law to provide preventive and supportive services.

In recent years, the Burger and Rehnquist Supreme Courts have imposed limitations that restrict lower federal courts from examining and correcting violations other than those of procedural due process. However, Juvenile Courts are still free to be, and duty bound to be, concerned with substantive justice. The charge to do so under law imposes a broad responsibility on judges to seek greater justice for youth.

To fulfill this charge judges will need to garner knowledge from many fields, as they seek more effective answers for the treatment of the young. They will have to learn more about the designated programs to which they send youths and about the consequences of their dispositions, whether foster home care, child-care institutions, jails, or a return to the child's family. They should report to the community on gaps and inadequacies in programs and in resources available for needed services.

In performing such responsibilities, judges will come to see themselves, not as distanced from youths but as advocates for youth. They can become powerful foes of every form of discrimination based on race, religion, or national origin.

Beyond these important functions, Juvenile Courts are in a position to demonstrate that the most pervasive and damaging form of discrimination against youth in this country arises from their poverty. What they do in this area could move legislatures and ultimately the judiciary to treat poverty as a suspect classification, subject to the special scrutiny now prescribed for cases involving racial discrimination.

Juvenile Courts cannot continue to function as a way station or a place of last resort if they are to make a significant contribution to youth. When families or the community fumble or fail youth, Juvenile Courts must develop ways to reverse a downward slide toward anger and despair. They must be enabled to ensure aid and human skill to alleviate pain and correct misbehavior.

Goals for Juvenile Justice in American Society

The vision of greater justice for neglected and delinquent children and youth can endure and grow only if America provides far more preventive and supportive services for all young people. If this country fails to do so, Juvenile Courts can only totter along until they become one more antique institution, fit only for historical comments.

Greater justice for youth cannot be separated from America's policies and practices that affect all youths in this country. The failure of the United

States to join other industrial western countries in providing a universal allowance for all children, as a matter of right, is at variance with its self-image of compassion and commitment to equal justice. In the absence of such an allowance to assure basic necessities, health care and education, formulas to require greater financial support by parents hold little promise for poor children.

National planning for the coordination and continuity of services for youth are essential to the achievement of justice. Leadership by the Federal government is needed to set standards, to monitor their implementation, to provide substantial funding, and to enforce compliance by all the programs it funds. It must reverse the Reagan policy of shifting responsibility to states, localities, private groups, and families. It must also use its leadership to encourage states and localities to more rather than less for youth at risk.

Apart from the responsibility for setting, monitoring, and enforcing standards for the care and treatment of youth, the Federal government should set the tone for how best to confront serious problems presented by youth. It should be open to new ideas but not a follower of fashionable trends as presented by shifts in funding programs for drug users, runaways, alcoholic, and now pregnant teenagers.

Only serious leadership can prevent yielding to the current demands for retribution, vengeance, and reincarceration as the answer to delinquent youth. It must search out the causes of maladjustment, delinquency, alienation, and violence practiced by youth. The tasks ahead are great and will not respond to any quick fixes. Americans can end the meanness of current programs for youth and reject as unworthy the cruel and futile recriminalization of younger and younger children.

Chapter Notes

Foreword

1 Nix, C. (1986, April 21). Unsettled lives: Growing up in city foster care. *The New York Times*, pp. B1, B4.

Preface

1 Tulin, L. A. (1928). The role of penalties in the criminal law. *Yale Law Journal, 37*(8), 1048-1069.

Chapter 1
Fifty Years of Changing Political Winds

1 Bremner, R. H. (1983). Other people's children. *Journal of Social History, 16*(3), 83-103.

2 Delinquency was loosely defined to include disobedience toward parents, truancy, misbehavior in the community and acts that would constitute a crime if committed by an adult.

3 Pinckney, M. W. (1912). Public pensions to widows. Experiences and observations which lead me to favor such a law. In R. H. Bremner, (Ed.), *Children and youth in America: A documentary history* (Vol. 2: 1866-1932, pp. 370-373). Cambridge, MA: Harvard University Press, 1971.

4 *In the matter of Higgins*, 46 Misc. 2d 233 (1965).

5 *Edwards v. California*, 314 U.S. 160 (1941).

6 Words of John Van Ness Yates, the New York Secretary of State (1823).

7 Bremner, R. H. (1983). op. cit., 83-103.

8 Tolchin, M. (1964, January 18). Experts wonder if family court is doing its job. *The New York Times*, p. 24.

9 Hoey, J. H. Federal Director of Public Assistance, "Memorandum to State Agencies" (Letter Number 43), December 2, 1944.

10 The Presiding Justice had enlisted in the armed services.

11 Letter from Acting Presiding Justice W. Bruce Cobb to Justine Wise Polier, June 7, 1943.

12 Letter from Acting Presiding Justice W. Bruce Cobb to Edwin Lucas, Director of the Society for the Prevention of Crime, November 28, 1945.

13 American Medical Association. (1922). *Journal of the American Medical Association, LXXVIII*, p. 1709. In R. H. Bremner, (Ed.), *Children and youth in America: A documentary history* (Vol. 2: 1866-1932, pp. 1020-1021). Cambridge, MA: Harvard University Press, 1971.

14 The National Lawyers Guild, The International Juridical Association, The Lawyers' Committee on American Relations with Spain.

15 *In the matter of Skipwith*, 14 Misc. 2nd 325, 180 N.Y.S. 2d 852 (1958). See chapter on racial discrimination.

16 *Shioutakon v. District of Columbia*, 236 F. 2d 666 (1956).

17 *People ex. rel. O'Connell v. Turner*, 55 Ill. 280 (1870).

18 *People v. Lewis*, 260 N.Y. 171 (1932).

19 Schinitsky, C. (1961, May). Observations with respect to children's court. Unpublished Domestic Relations Court Committee Memorandum Report. Association of the Bar of the City of New York.

20 Schinitsky, C. (1962, January). The role of the lawyer in children's court. *Bar Bulletin*, Association of the Bar of the City of New York.

21 *Kent v. U.S.*, 383 U.S. 541 (1966).

22 *In re Gault*, 387 U.S. 1 (1967).

23 *In re Winship*, 397 U.S. 358 (1970).

24 *McKeiver v. Pennsylvania*, 403 U.S. 528 (1971). [Justices Black, Douglas, and Marshall dissenting.]

25 Knitzer, J. (1984). *Law guardians in New York State: A study of the legal representation of children.* Albany: New York State Bar Association. This study, of counsel in the Juvenile Court in New York State outside New York City, found 45% of counsel seriously or marginally inadequate, 27% acceptable, but only 4% effective.

26 Harrison, E. (1961, May 15). Ribicoff reports drift in welfare. *The New York Times*, p. 16.

27 Stetson, D. (1961, May 11). Nixon criticizes cost of welfare. *The New York Times*, pp. 1, 26.

28 Wickenden, E. (1971, May 4). *Back to the Poor Law via Section 1115.* Informational memorandum prepared for the Forum on Social Issues and Policies. National Assembly for Social Policy and Development (photocopied).

29 Semple, R. B., Jr. (1971, April 3). Nixon stays California welfare cutoff. *The New York Times*, p. 9.

30 Schmeck, H. M., Jr. (1973, July 27). A billion in health funds found unspent by H.E.W. *The New York Times*, pp. 1, 12.

31 Dr. Frederick C. Green, Associate Chief of the U.S. Children's Bureau, Department of Health, Education and Welfare, resigned in May 1973.

32 Moynihan, D. P. (1968, May). The Democrats, Kennedy and the murder of Dr. King. *Commentary.* Quoted in Schlesinger, A. M., Jr. *Robert Kennedy and his times* (p. 797). Boston: Houghton-Mifflin Co. 1978.

33 Zigler, E. F. (1974, July). Op-Ed *The New York Times*.

34 Tribe, L. H. (1979). *1979 supplement to American constitutional law*. Mineola, NY: Foundation Press.

35 Kristol, I. (1978, September 18). Human nature and social reform. *The Wall Street Journal*, p. 22.

36 *The New York Times*. (1981, January).

37 Wheeler, R. (1979, April 30). *Hunger in America: Ten years later*. Testimony before the Subcommittee on Nutrition, Senate Committee on Agriculture, Nutrition and Forestry. Washington, DC: U.S. Government Printing Office.

38 Brenner, H. (1976). *Estimating the social costs of national economic policy.* Washington, DC: U.S. Government Printing Office.

39 Ohlin, L. E. (1983). The future of juvenile justice policy and research. *Crime and Delinquency, 29*(3), 463-472.

40 Rivlin, A. (1983, April 28). Testimony of Director, Congressional Budget Office, before Select Committee on Children, Youth, and Families, U.S. House of Representatives.

41 Congressional Research Service, A Congressional Office Report, 1983.

42 Malcolm, A. (1985, October 20). New generation of poor youths emerges in U.S. *The New York Times*, pp. 1, 56.

43 *Hamilton v. Love*, 328 F. Supp. 1182 (E.D. Arkansas 1971).

Chapter 2
For Delinquents: The Tail End of Justice

1 MHS Proceedings. (1887-1889). Journey of Josiah Quincy through southern parts of New England, 1801. In R. H. Bremner, (Ed.), *Children and youth in America: A documentary history* (Vol. 1: 1600-1865, p. 174). Cambridge, MA: Harvard University Press, 1970.

2 The Family Standards Act was finally upheld by the U.S. Supreme Court in 1941.

3 Such discriminatory reactions persisted. A Massachusetts study of juvenile justice in 1979 reported that delinquent youth from "better families" were more likely to be placed in the better facilities and, as a rule, were placed for shorter periods.

4 Letter from New York State Department of Social Services to New York City Department of Welfare, September 17, 1954.

5 Letter from New York City Department of Welfare to Chief Probation Officer, January 4, 1956.

6 Memoranda, January 18, 1943 and March 5, 1945.

7 *Report of the President's Commission on Law Enforcement and the Administration of Justice*. (1967). Washington, DC: U.S. Government Printing Office.

8 Empey, L. T. (1978). *American delinquency: Its meaning and construction* (p. 460). Homewood, IL: Dorsey Press.

9 U.S. Department of Justice, Law Enforcement Assistance Administration (LEAA). (1978). *Children in custody: Advance report on the 1977 census of public juvenile facilities* (No. SD-JD-5A). Washington, DC: U.S. Government Printing Office.

10 U.S. Department of Justice, Law Enforcement Assistance Administration (LEAA). (1979). *Juvenile justice program models*. Washington, DC: U.S. Government Printing Office.

11 Polk, K. (1984). Juvenile diversion: A look at the record. *Crime and Delinquency, 30*, 648-658.

12 Little, A. D., Inc. (1977). *Response to angry youth*. U.S. Department of Justice, Law Enforcement Assistance Administration. Washington, DC: U.S. Government Printing Office.

13 See *A preliminary study of adolescent murderers*, presented at the 27th Annual Meeting of the Canadian Psychiatric Association, September 1977.

14 Confidentiality regulations forbade reviewing information recorded after 1972.

15 Hofstadter, R. (1976). Reflections on violence in the United States. In R.Hofstadter & M. Wallace (Eds.), *American violence* (pp. 3-43). New York: Vantage Books.

16 Roddy, J. (1979). Juvenile aversion therapy: Counter-clockwork constitutional violations. *Juvenile and Family Court Journal, 30*(4), 17-38.

17 Hofstadter, R. (1976). op. cit., pp. 26-27.

18 ibid.

19 Schmidt, W. E. (1986, November 5). Wider pattern of gang violence seen. *The New York Times*, p. A14.

20 Juvenile Reform Act of (1976). Legislation to improve state facilities was defeated in the same term.

21 *Breed v. Jones.* (1975, May 27). *U.S. Law Week, 43*(46), 4644-4651.

22 Letter from William Sheridan, Consultant to the Children's Bureau, November 12, 1952.

23 Chambers, M. (1986, October 13). Concern about youths in adult jails. *The New York Times*, p. A15.

24 Lewis, D. O. & Balla, D. (1976). *Delinquency and psychopathology.* New York: Grune & Stratton.

25 *Schall v. Martin,* 467 U.S. 253 (1984).

26 Dembitz, N. (1975, February 5). Treatment of dangerous delinquents. *New York Law Journal,* 1, 7.

27 *In re welfare of J.E.C.,* 225 N.W. 2d 245 (1975).

28 Currie, E. (1985). *Confronting crime: An American challenge* (p. 10). New York: Pantheon Books.

29 Bazelon, D. (1980, October 19). [Letter to the Editor]. *The New York Times*, p. 20E.

Chapter 3
The Drive for Punishment: Violence Against Youth

1 Finagrette, H. (1980). Law and punishment. *The Center Magazine, 13*(1),42-50.

2 Oelsner, L. (1974, February 15). U.S. bars crime fund use on behavior modification. *The New York Times*, p. 66.

3 In 1974, the Federal government halted its LEAA-sponsored programs for the systematic modification of behavior of institutional inmates, including juveniles and alcoholics; see Oelsner (1974).

4 Bentham, J. (1948). *An introduction to the principles of morals and legislation* (pp. 16-17). New York: Hafner Press.

5 Durkheim, E. (1964). *Rules of sociological method* (p.36). New York: The Free Press.

6 Kean, A.W.G. (1937). The history of the criminal liability of children. *The Law Quarterly Review, 53*(211), 364-370.

7 De Beaumont, G. & de Tocqueville, A. (1833). On the penitentiary system in the United States and its application in France; with an appendix on penal colonies and also statistical notes (F. Lieber, trans.). In R. H. Bremner, (Ed.), *Children and youth in America: A documentary history* (Vol. 1: 1600-1865, pp. 683- 685). Cambridge, MA: Harvard University Press, 1970.

8 *People ex. rel. O'Connell v. Turner*, 55 Ill. 280 (1870).

9 Of the youths in need of placement, 20% were black, and insufficient foster homes were recruited by the agencies.

10 Gardner, G. E. (1951). *The institution as therapist*. Speech given at Berkshire Farms Institute Forum. Published 1952 in *The Child, 16*(5), 70-72.

11 Citizens' Commission to Investigate Corporal Punishment in Junior High School 22. (1974). *Corporal punishment and school suspensions: A case study* (monograph). New York: Metropolitan Applied Research Center (MARC).

12 Letter from Bettina Warburg, MD to Justine Wise Polier, May 9, 1951.

13 Gil, D. G. (1973). *Violence against children*. Cambridge, MA: Harvard University Press.

14 Letter to Justine Wise Polier, August 3, 1944.

15 Deutsch, A. (1947, June 22). *P.M.*

16 Defeated in 1953, this legislation was reintroduced in 1954.

17 Polier, J. W. (1952, April 29). [Letter to the Editor]. *The New York Times*, p. 26.

18 Brown, L. (1975, March). *Issues of drugging in schooling*. Paper presented at the Annual Meeting of the American Orthopsychiatric Association, Washington, DC.

19 Kroll, J. L. (1977). The concept of childhood in the middle ages. *Journal of the History of the Behavioral Sciences, 13*(4), 384-393.

Chapter 4
Neglected and Abused Children

1 Schwabacher, E. (1979, October 14). *Personal journal* (Vol. 5: 1979-80, p. 119). Unpublished manuscript.

2 *Smith v. Williams*, 13 N.Y. Misc. 761 (1895).

3 Hart, H. H. (1884). Placing out children in the west. In R. H. Bremner (Ed.), *Children and youth in America: A documentary history* (Vol. 2: 1866-1932, pp. 305-309). Cambridge, MA: Harvard University Press, 1971.

4 State Charities Aid Association Report, (1961).

5 Polansky, N. A., Hally, C. & Polansky, N. F. (1971). *Profile of neglect*. Washington, DC: Public Service Administration, Department of Health, Education and Welfare.

6 *In the matter of Marion Francis*, 267 N.Y.S. 2d 566, 49 Misc. 2d 372 (1966).

7 Gil, D. (1973, March 26). Testimony before Subcommittee on Child Abuse, U.S. Senate.

8 Blair, J. & Duncan, D. F. (1977). Child abuse as a work-related problem. *Corrective and Social Psychiatry and Journal of Behavior Technology, Method and Therapy, 23*(2), 53-55.

9 In New York City, the numbers rose rapidly when reporting of abuse was required, and a central state registry was established in the early 1970s.

10 Public Law 93-247, 92nd Congress, S1197.

11 Brown, B. S. (1977). Foreword to *Child abuse and neglect programs: Practice and theory* (GPO 78-344). New York: Community Research Applications, Inc.

12 Hall, B. (1980). Sexual victimization and juvenile prostitution. Citing the Delancy Street Foundation of San Francisco. In *Perspectives*, Region VI Resource Center on Child Abuse and Neglect, University of Texas at Austin.

13 Rieker, P. P. & Carmen, E. H. (1986). The victim to patient process: The disconfirmation and transformation of abuse. *American Journal of Orthopsychiatry, 56*(3), 360-370.

14 Region VI Resource Center on Child Abuse and Neglect. (1980). Seminar at the University of Texas at Austin.

15 Butler, S. (1939). *The way of all flesh* (p.278). New York: Washington Square Press.

16 The suicide rate among 15- to 24-year-olds tripled from 1955 to 1973 and had become the leading cause of death in this age group.

17 Deardorff, N. & Robison, S. (1937). *The organization of services for behavior problem children* (pp. 28-31). Unpublished manuscript.

18 Letter from three major sectarian federations to the Presiding Justice, February 2, 1937.

19 Staff was supported by a grant from Marshall Field.

20 Polier, J. W. (1964). *A view from the bench.* Paramus, NJ: National Council on Crime and Delinquency.

21 Festinger, T. (1985). *No one ever asked us: a postscript to foster care.* New York: Columbia University Press.

Chapter 5
The Search for Permanence

1 American Academy of Pediatrics, Bureau of Child Hygiene—New York City Health Department and the Citizens' Committee for Children of New York, Inc. 1948.

2 Mayor's Task Force on Child Care. (1974, November 8). *Draft report*. New York.

3 The Children's Defense Fund. (1976). *Children in adult jails* (pp. 27-37). Washington, DC: The Washington Research Project.

4 Maas, H. S. & Engler, R. B. (1959). *Children in need of parents*. New York: Columbia University Press.

5 Chs. 448, 449, 450, N.Y. Laws of 1959, effective April 15, 1959. Family Court Act, Article 6, Section 611 d., 622.

6 Polier, S. (1959). Amendments to New York's adoption law: The permanently neglected child. *Child Welfare, 38*(7), 1-4.

7 New York, (1971). Ch. 901; Family Court Act, Section 611.

8 New York, (1973). Ch. 870; Sec.1, Family Court Act, Article 6, Section 617, 621, 831, 1043.

9 New York, (1973). Ch. 863; Social Service Law, Section 384 (b)(4)(c).

10 Family Court Act, Section 1055; Social Service Law, Section 384-G (e)(b), Section 392.

11 In 1975, most states had still not recognized the standing of foster parents to participate in termination proceedings.

12 Levine, R. S. (1975). Foundations for drafting a model statute to terminate parental rights: A selected bibliography. *Juvenile Justice, 26*(3), 42-56.

13 The required 18 months of continuing care as a condition of foster parents' action was reduced to 12 months in 1973.

14 New York, 1973, Social Service Law, Ch. 940, Section 398; Family Court Act, Ch. 901, Section 615.

15 *In the matter of Hime, Y.*, 425 NYS 2d 336 (1980).

16 See *In the matter of Hime, Y.*, 425 NYS 2d 336 (1980). The judge also terminated the right of a sibling while granting right of visitation to this mother.

17 *In the matter of Sanjivini, K.*, (1978, June 28). *New York Law Journal*, 12-13.

18 *In the matter of Jennifer S.*, 330 NYS 2d 872 (1972).

19 *In re J.C.*, 251 S.E. 2d 299 (1978).

20 *In the matter of Doe*, 636 P. 2d 888 (N.M. Ct. App. 1981).

21 Goldstein, J., Freud, A. & Solnit, A. J. (1973). *Beyond the best interests of the child.* New York: The Free Press.

22 Goldstein, J., Freud, A. & Solnit, A. J. (1979). *Before the best interests of the child.* New York: The Free Press.

23 ibid. (Footnote, p. 3).

24 Writing about the earlier volume, Alfred Kadushin (1974), a distinguished leader in the child welfare field, pointed out that social workers rarely have the luxury of choosing between the "good, better and best," but rather are forced daily to choose between the "bad, worse and worst."

25 Kadushin, A. (1974). Beyond the best interests of the child: An essay review. *Social Service Review*, 48(4), 508-516.

26 Letter from Brenda Kelly to Justine Wise Polier, November 24, 1980.

27 *New England Home for Little Wanderers v. Sylvander.* 328 N.E. 2d 854 (1975).

28 The groups were the American Orthopsychiatric Association; the Association for Children of New Jersey; the Child Welfare League of America, Inc.; the Children's Defense Fund; the Institute for Child Advocacy; the National Association of Social Workers; the New York State Citizens' Coalition for Children; the North American Council for Adoptable Children; and the Youth Policy and Law Center. The brief was filed June 6, 1980.

29 In the same year, the U.S. Supreme Court held that the proof of parental failure sig-
    nificant to warrant termination must be clear and convincing, but did not have to
    be beyond a reasonable doubt. See *Santosky v. Kramer* (1982).

30 *Santosky v. Kramer*, 455 U.S. 745 (1982).

31 Letter from Frank Farro, Associate Chief, U.S. Children's Bureau, to Justine Wise
    Polier, March 9, 1979.

32 Katz, S. N. (1978). Freeing children for permanent placement through a model act.
    Family Law Quarterly, 12(3), 203-251.

Chapter 6
The Unmarried Mother, Illegitimacy, and Adoption

1 *In re Braun*, 145 N.W. 2d 482 (1966).

2 William L. Mitchell, Commissioner of Social Security, stated in January 1966 that
   "Little is known abut the problems and needs of the large numbers of these children
   who do not receive public aid, although there is reason to believe many are in homes
   of meager income."

3 *Baltimore Sun* (1964, January 19).

4 *Levy v. Louisiana*, 391 U.S. 68 (1968) [Justice Rehnquist dissenting].

5 *Glona v. American Guarantee Company*, 391 U.S. 73 (1968) [Justices Brennan,
   White and Marshall dissenting].

6 *Labine v. Vincent*, 401 U.S. 532 (1971).

7 *King v. Smith*, 392 U.S. 309 (1968).

8 *Trimble v. Gordon*, 430 U.S. 762 (1977).

9 *Fiallo v. Bell*, 430 U.S. 787 (1977) [Justices Marshall, Brennan and White dissent-
   ing].

10 *Califano v. Boles*, 443 U.S. 282 (1979).

11 *Doe v. Shapiro*, 302 F. Supp. 761 (D. Conn. 1969); appeal dismissed 396 U.S. 488 (1970); *Doe v. Harder*, 310 F. Supp. 302 (D. Conn. 1970); appeal dismissed 399 U.S. 902 (1970).

12 Ch. 911, Conn. General Statutes, Sec. 52-440 (b).

13 *Welfare Commissioner v. Stone*, Circuit Ct., 1st Circuit, Conn., Hon. G. S. Ford, January 28, 1974. See *Roe v. Norton* (1975), *amicus* brief, Appendix A.

14 *Roe v. Norton*, 422 U.S. 391 (1975). Marion W. Edelman and Justine Wise Polier, attorneys. 365 F. Supp. 65 (D. Conn. 1973).

15 *Matter of Johnson*, Domestic Rel. Ct. N.Y. County (1938).

16 Memorandum from Assistant Director, Louise Wise Services to Shad Polier, April 4, 1970.

17 Krause, H. D. (1971). *Illegitimacy, law and social policy* (p. ix). New York: Bobbs-Merrill.

18 Massachusetts Civil Law, 1932; North Carolina Civil Code, 1935; Pennsylvania Public Law, 1939.

19 Thirty-one states authorized such action when a child was adopted.

20 Rivlin, A. (1983, April 28). Testimony of Director, Congressional Budget Office, before Select Committee on Children, Youth, and Families, U.S. House of Representatives.

21 Quoted by Michael Foot. (1981). *Debts of honour* (p. 121). New York: Harper & Row.

22 Massachusetts was the first state to establish statutory adoption in 1851. Most states followed by 1900.

23 Louise Wise Services, renamed in honor of its founder.

24 *In re Jewish Child Care Association*, 5 N.Y. 2d 222, 183 N.Y.S. 2d 65 (1959).

25 Fanshel, D. (1982). *On the road to permanency: An expanded data base for service to children in foster care* (p. 243, 1979 interim report. Final report 1982). New York: Child Welfare League of America, Inc.

26 P.L. 90-272 (1980). This Act also extended Medicaid to cover children with special needs.

27 *Alma Society v. Mellon*, 601 F. 2d 1225 2d (1979), 444 U.S. 995 (1979). The U.S. Supreme Court denied certiorari.

28 *Stanley v. Illinois*, 405 U.S. 645 (1972).

29 Morlock, M. (1939). Washington, DC: U.S. Children's Bureau.

Chapter 7
Sex and the Double Standard

1 Report from Bellevue Hospital, September 25, 1939, signed by Lauretta Bender, MD, Senior Psychiatrist, and by Karl M. Bowman, Director.

2 Institute of Judicial Administration—American Bar Association. Joint Commission on Juvenile Justice Standards. (1977). Statutory grounds for intervention. In Juvenile Justice Standards Project, *Standards relating to abuse and neglect* (Part II, pp. 60-75). Cambridge, MA: Ballinger.

3 Kempe, R. S. & Kempe, C. H. (1978). *Child abuse* (pp. 43- 56, 103). Cambridge, MA: Harvard University Press.

4 Fairbank, J. K. (1979). *The United States and China* (4th rev. ed., pp. 23, 121). Cambridge, MA: Harvard University Press.

5 Mitterrand frees 21 jailed mothers. (1981, August 13). *The New York Times*, p. A9.

6 New York City Department of Welfare, Memorandum, December 3, 1945.

7 Laws of 1951, Ch. 716, effective June 1, 1951.

8 Presidential Message to Congress, 1935.

9 *Califano v. Wescott*, 443 U.S. 76 (1979).

10 *King v. Smith*, 392 U.S. 309 (1968).

11 Following the Supreme Court decision in *King*, 15 states abolished statutes requiring "suitable" homes as a condition for aid to children residing with their mothers.

12 Ginsberg, M. (1969, September 24). *Review of AFDC N.Y.C.* [Mimeographed Report].

13 Wickenden, E. (1965, March 23). *Poverty and the law: The constitutional rights of assistance recipients.* Memorandum to the National Social Welfare Assembly.

14 Rutter, M. (1976). Parent-child separation: Psychological effects on the children. In A. M. Clarke & A. D. B. Clarke (Eds.), *Early experience: Myth and evidence* (pp. 153-186). New York: The Free Press.

15 Pifer, A. (1976). *Women working: Toward a new society* (pp. 3-18). New York: The Carnegie Corp.

16 Price, R. R. (1977). The forgotten female offender. *Crime and Delinquency, 23*(2), 101.

Chapter 8
The Ups and Downs of Mental Health

1 Reich, C. (1965). Toward the humanistic study of law. *Yale Law Journal, 74*(7), 1402, 1405.

2 Camus, A. (1969). *Summer in Algeria*, p. 87. New York: Knopf.

3 Goddard offered proof from tests he had given to immigrants to show that 87% of the Russians, 82% of the Jews, 80% of the Hungarians, and 79% of the Italian immigrants were feeble-minded.

4 Davis, A. (1976). Public controversy over mental testing. In Frankel, C. (Ed.) *Controversies and decisions: The social services and public policy* (p. 132). New York: Russell Sage Foundation.

5 Kamin, L. J. (1974). *The science and politics of IQ.* Potomac, MD, NJ: Lawrence Erlbaum.

6 Report from Director of Adolescent Unit at Brooklyn Hospital.

7 At the New York City Board of Education's Child Guidance Clinic Harlem Unit, Dr. Max Winsor and Dr. Viola W. Bernard collected basic information in the early 1940s.

8 Joint Advisory Committee, N.Y.C Board of Education. (1949). *The role of the school in preventing and correcting maladjustment and delinquency: A study in three schools*. New York: N.Y.C. Board of Education. (Monograph Report of the Research Committee.) The project was funded by the New York Foundation and the Hofheimer Fund. Frank J. O'Brien, MD and Marion E. Kenworthy, MD co-chaired the Joint Advisory Committee and Justine Wise Polier chaired the Research Committee. The report was completed in December of 1947 and published in February 1949.

9 The annual budget of $11,000 was provided successively over 8 years by Doris Duke, Eugene Meyer, and Marshall Field. The program included an outstanding supervisor, Virginia Bellsmith, to train the graduate students.

10 Peck, H. B., Harrower, M. & Beck, M. B. (1958). *A new pattern for mental health services in a children's court* (pp. 50-59). Springfield, IL: Charles C. Thomas.

11 Deutsch, A. (1959). *The story of GAP*. New York: Group for the Advancement of Psychiatry.

12 Polier, J. W. (1968). *The rule of law and the role of psychiatry*. Baltimore, MD: Johns Hopkins University Press.

13 American Psychiatric Association. (n.d.). *Official position statements of the American Psychiatric Association in precis form, 1948-1975*. Washington, DC: American Psychiatric Association.

14 Joint Commission on Mental Illness and Health. (1961). *Action for mental health: Final report of the Joint Commission on Mental Illness and Health*. New York: Basic Books.

15 Joint Commission on Mental Health of Children. (1970). *Crisis in child mental health: Challenge for the 1970's*. New York: Harper & Row. (Because the earlier Joint Commission's report had given short shrift to the mental health needs of children, Congress commissioned a new study specifically focusing on children and youth.)

16 The President's Commission on Mental Health. (1978). *Report to the President from the President's Commission on Mental Health* (Vols. 1-4). Washington, DC: U.S. Government Printing Office.

17 *Rouse v. Cameron*, 373 F. 2d 451, 459 (1966).

18 *Wyatt v. Stickney*, 325 F. Supp. 781, 785 (M.D. Alabama 1971); 344 F. Supp. 373 (M.D. Alabama 1972).

19 In this decision the court stated that when a person was deprived of liberty for therapeutic reasons, the failure to provide appropriate treatment violated "the very fundament of due process." See *Wyatt v. Stickney* (1971).

20 *Morales v. Turman*, 383 F. Supp. 53 (E.D. Texas 1974).

21 *O'Connor v. Donaldson*, 422 U.S. 563 (1975).

22 It was not until 1986 that six states began to modify the requirements that only dangerous persons could be hospitalized involuntarily. See Goleman (1986).

23 Goleman, D. (1986, December 9). States move to ease law committing mentally ill. *The New York Times*, pp. C1, C4.

24 *McKeiver v. Pennsylvania*, 403 U.S. 528 (1971).

25 *Dixon v. Weinberger*, 405 F. Supp. 974 (1975).

26 Joint Commission on Mental Health of Children. (1970). op. cit.

27 Kenworthy, M. E. (1962). *Report of the Subcommittee on Mental Health Services of the Citizens' Committee for the Domestic Relations Court of the City of New York* (Mimeographed).

28 Report by Justine Wise Polier to Justice Bernard Botein. April 22, 1968. *Report on Mental Health Services in the Family Court of the City of New York* (Mimeographed).

29 Makover, H. B. (1966). *Mental health services in the family court of the State of New York in the City of New York* (Mimeographed).

30 Committee on Mental Health Services Inside and Outside the Court. (1972). *Juvenile justice confounded: Pretensions and realities of treatment services.* Paramus, NJ.: National Council on Crime and Delinquency.

31 Kalogerakis, M. (1977). Personal communication, June 4.

32 *Rogers v. Okin,* 478 F. Supp. 1342 (D. Mass. 1979).

33 Hersch, S. P. (1978). *Annual report of child and adolescent programs of the National Institute of Mental Health.* Unpublished.

34 Bernard, V. W., & Abbate, G. M. (1964). *Report of the department of hospitals' committee on psychiatric services for children to the commissioner of hospitals, New York City.* New York: New York City Community Mental Health Board.

35 Minutes, "State Department of Mental Health and Family Court Committee on Mental Health," February 21, 1971.

36 Committee on Mental Health Services Inside and Outside the Court. (1972). op. cit.

37 Hearing, May 31, 1966.

38 *Bartley v. Kremens,* 402 F. Supp. 1039 (E.D. Penn. 1975).

39 *Parham v. J.R.,* 442 U.S. 584 (1979).

40 Knitzer, J. (1982). *Unclaimed children: The failure of public responsibility to children and adolescents in need of mental health services.* Washington, DC: Children's Defense Fund.

41 *Hobson v. Hansen,* 269 F. Supp. 401 (1967).

42 *Larry P. v. Wilson Riles,* 495 F. Supp. 926 (1979).

43 *Ingraham v. Wright,* 430 U.S. 651 (1977).

44 *Pennhurst v. Halderman,* 465 U.S. 89 (1984).

45 *City of New York et al. v. Margaret M. Heckler,* 742 F. 2d 729 (1984). [Sustained on appeal to the U.S. Supreme Court.]

46 Taylor, S., Jr. (1986, June 3). High court backs mentally ill on benefit suits. *The New York Times*, pp. A1, D27.

47 U.S. Department of Health and Human Services. (1981, December). *8th annual report on children and youth activities* (p. 72).

48 Schmeck, H. M., Jr. (1984, October 3). Almost one in 5 may have mental illness. *The New York Times*, pp. A1, D27. (The news report is based on a study published in the *Archives of General Psychiatry*.)

49 Lamb, H. R. (Ed.). (1984). The homeless mentally ill: A task force report of the American Psychiatric Association. Washington, DC: The American Psychiatric Association.

Chapter 9
Religious Separatism

1 Pfeffer, Leo. (1965). *The liberties of an American* (p. 32). Boston: Beacon Press.

2 Bryce, J. (1889). *The American commonwealth*. London: Macmillan.

3 Administrative Code, City of New York, Title B, Subsection 603.6.0 (1946).

4 Wicklein, J. (1959, October 11). Religious rule on adoption bars many couples in state. *The New York Times*, pp. 1, 82.

5 Report on Conference at Villanova, Pennsylvania School of Law. (1957, March 30). *The Brooklyn Tablet*.

6 *In re Vardinakis et al.*, 289 N.Y.S. 355, 160 Misc. 13 (1936).

7 Polier, J. W. (1975). Professional abuse of children. *American Journal of Orthopsychiatry, 45*(3), 357-362.

8 Letter, June 30, 1955.

9 Protests by the Probation Union and the NAACP were ignored. The Board of Justices in New York City supported the legislation, with a minority dissenting.

10 *In the matter of Santos*, Domestic Relations Court, #755/6 (1949).

11 Sicher, Hon. Dudley. Opinion, March 19, 1951.

12 *In the matter of Santos*, 278 App. Div. 373, 105 N.Y.S. 2d 716 (1951).

13 Memorandum from the Chief Probation Officer, New York Juvenile Court, May 16, 1951.

Chapter 10
Racial Discrimination

1 Starrs, J. E. (1967). Southern juvenile courts—A study of irony, civil rights, and judicial practice. *Crime and Delinquency 13*(2), 305.

2 See Starrs (1967). He also warned that the faith of blacks in the Supreme Court, after *Brown*, had been misplaced.

3 Evans, A. (Ed.). (1940). *Directory of social and health agencies of New York City.* Community Council of Greater New York, Inc. New York: Columbia University Press.

4 Twenty-three Protestant and 23 Catholic agencies accepted only white children in 1939.

5 Letter from Frederick W. Ecker, President of Children's Village Board of Directors, to Rev. Shelton Hale Bishop, July 31, 1941.

6 Service Bureau for Negro Children under the Children's Aid Society, supported by Marshall Field.

7 Cox, W. B., Shelly, J. A., & Minard, G. C. (Eds). (1940). *Handbook of American institutions for delinquent juveniles, Vol. 2: Kentucky/Tennessee.* New York: The Osborne Association.

8 P.S. 10. Blacks constituted 80% of the 46,000 persons living within the 26 blocks of the school district that included this school.

9 Drafted by Shad Polier and amended to exempt any religious institution.

10 Letter from William Hodson, Commissioner of the New York City Department of Welfare, to Mayor Fiorello LaGuardia, October 14, 1942.

11 Blake-Quimby Report to Foster Care Commission, (1948).

12 Blake-Quimby Report, ibid.

13 Letter from Justine Wise Polier to Rev. Leland Henry, January 30, 1947.

14 Hillcrest Center for Children. (1964). *Eighth annual report.* Bedford Hills, NY: Hillcrest Center for Children.

15 Financed by the Field Foundation.

16 Patricia Garland Morisey, PhD.

17 Letter from New York City Department of Welfare, September 29, 1961.

18 Letter from Carol Parry, October 17, 1974.

19 Article 6.

20 New York State Family Court Act, Laws of 1962, Ch. 686.

21 *In re Ellen Bonez,* 272 N.Y.S. 2d 587 (1966).

22 Civil Rights Act of 1964, Title VI.

23 U.S. Department of Health, Education and Welfare, Office of Education. (1966). *Equality of educational opportunity.* Washington, DC: U.S. Government Printing Office.

24 Para un nuevo dia en la educacion: The Chicano Education Project. (1978). *Carnegie Quarterly, 26*(1), 1-6.

25 Memorandum from Chief Probation Officer Lindgren, (1938, on the closing by Gould, Colored Orphan Asylum, Five Points, and Children's Aid Society.

26 Memorandum, Court Committee on Institutions, December, 1940.

27 Committee on Mental Health Services Inside and Outside the Court. (1972). *Juvenile justice confounded: Pretensions and realities of treatment services.* Paramus, NJ.: National Council on Crime and Delinquency.

28 The private agencies had also accepted only 14% of minority-group children, but 67% of white children, involved in drug abuse.

29 Lewis, D. O., Balla, D. A., & Shanok, S. S. (1979). Some evidence of race bias in the diagnosis and treatment of the juvenile offender. *American Journal of Orthopsychiatry, 49*(1), 53-61.

30 *In the matter of Skipwith and Rector*, 14 Misc. 2d 325; 180 N.Y.S. 2d 852 (1958).

31 *Wilder v. Sugarman*, 385 F. Supp. 1013 (S.D.N.Y. 1974) [3–judge court].

32 Of 6,170 children in the care of its member agencies in 1973, only 430 were white children.

33 Plaintiffs had reserved the right to appeal an earlier Federal decision that the New York law was not unconstitutional on its face.

34 *Wilder v. Bernstein*, 645 F. Supp. 1292 (S.D.N.Y. 1986) [Appeal pending].

35 U.S. Department of Justice, Law Enforcement Assistance Administration. (1980). *Children in custody: Advance report on the 1979 census of public juvenile facilities.* Washington, DC: U.S. Government Printing Office.

36 Rule, S. (1978, November 17). New juvenile unit on Rikers: A view from within. *The New York Times*, p. B3.

37 Wright, J. S. (1978, December 8-9). Presentation at Symposium on Southern Civil Rights, Dillard University.

Index

Page numbers in *italics* indicate Chapter Notes.